Backcountry Access Guide

Ken Lans, Editor

The Washington Backcountry Access Guide is designed to give you the facts you need about access, regulations, permits, user fees, and requirements that apply to wilderness areas throughout Washington State. You'll also find complete contact information for land managers, ranger stations, wilderness information centers, road, weather, and avalanche information, as well as other useful information such as trail problems and closures.

Within the limitations imposed by production schedules and print deadlines, the *Access Guide* contains the most recent information available from each of the areas covered. In most cases, this means information available as of late February 1998. Where late-breaking changes are expected, we've made special note so you can be sure to contact the appropriate agency or ranger district as you plan your trip.

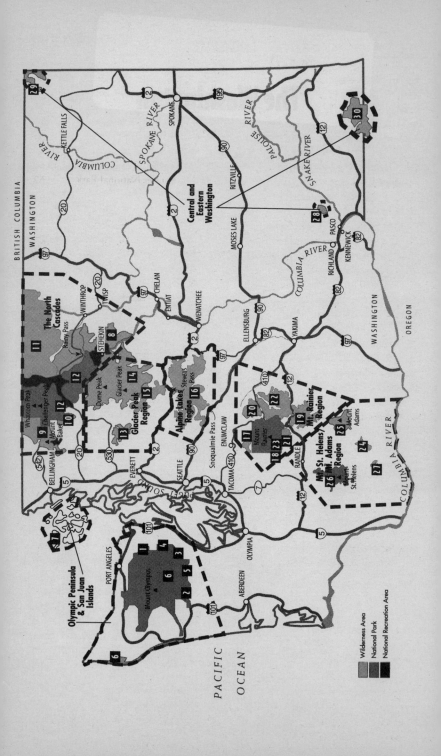

Contents

Acknowledgments

Publications like the *Washington Backcountry Access Guide* result from the combined efforts of many people.

The land managers who have jurisdiction over Washington's wilderness areas, and its national forests, parks, monuments, and recreation areas have wholeheartedly supported this publication and contributed and gave their stamps of approval to the information covering their respective areas. They provided valuable advice, supplied facts and information, and reviewed and proofread drafts. Their professional and enthusiastic efforts to both protect wild areas and make them available for public use are much appreciated and we hope this book will help them in their work.

Pete Clitherow investigated how to get places without a car and John Roper supplied the Bulger's list of 100 highest Washington peaks. Members of the Mountaineers staff provided invaluable help and support, including: Rick Bishop, Steve Costie, Brooke Drury, Matt Golec, Alison Huffman, and Geof Logan.

Remember to have fun when you head into the mountains. Renew yourself and revel in the grandeur—but also take the time to get down on your hands and knees and marvel in tiny clumps of moss and lichen and rivulets of water dancing in the streams. It's not just the looming peaks that make wilderness the special place it is. It's also the myriad of small wonders and unexpected details that snag our hearts, excite our spirits, and illuminate our souls. Be safe and responsible and help keep these wild areas magical and intact for the generations yet to come.

—*Ken Lans*

Access Guide Updates Online
http://www.mountaineers.org/

Things change. In many cases information on permits, regulations, quota areas, and fees was incomplete or unknown when we went to press. We'll make up-to-date information available on The Mountaineers Web site and include any other major changes that may occur. If you know of any we miss, contact us at one of the addresses listed below.

Advance Scouts Needed

We've done our best to make this *Access Guide* as useful, current, and accurate as we could. You can help make future editions even better. If you come across information that is wrong, confusing, or misleading, let us know. If you have suggestions for information or items you'd like to see in our next edition, we'd be happy to consider them for publication. Send your corrections, tips, suggestions, comments, and submissions to:

Backcountry Access Guide
The Mountaineers
300 Third Avenue West
Seattle, WA 98119
e-mail: *clubmail@mountaineers.org*

Planning Your Backcountry Trip

The *Washington Backcountry Access Guide* is a complement to the growing selection of excellent regional hiking guides that provide trail and trip descriptions and help you decide where you might want to go. This book, by collecting most of the information you'll need to plan your trip in one convenient, easy-to-use package, will answer most other planning questions you might have.

WHO'S IN CHARGE?

The map at the front identifies the locations of the national parks, national recreation areas, and wilderness areas in Washington. This *Access Guide* will help you figure out which agency has jurisdiction over the areas you're visiting. While books, including this one, are a good starting point, it's always a wise idea to contact, by phone or in person, the agency managing the area you wish to visit (e.g., ranger districts in National Forests) for the most accurate and current information, especially on road and trail conditions and closures.

Note that more than one national forest may administer a wilderness area; national forests are further subdivided into ranger districts, which manage different sections of a wilderness. We've included names, addresses, and telephone numbers for U.S. Forest Service ranger districts, National Park Service wilderness information centers, visitor centers, and ranger stations, Bureau of Land Management regional offices, and U.S. Fish and Wildlife Service administrative offices. When you call, be sure to tell agency staff you're using this *Access Guide* and ask if they have any updates you should know about.

DO YOU NEED A PERMIT?

With the increasingly heavy use of Washington's backcountry and wild areas, many national forests and national parks are now using permits and quotas to limit, control, and track entry into wilderness areas and/or are requiring overnight users to camp in designated sites. While limiting entry is still not the norm, a few especially heavily used areas now have reservation systems for overnight stays, and most areas either request trailhead registration or require backcountry permits for overnight and/or day use.

The type of permit you need depends on how long you'll stay and where you'll be going. Day-use and overnight permits can be obtained at ranger stations and information centers and both may often be obtained at trailheads as well. The listings for each area tell you whether use quotas exist and what permits are required—day use, overnight use, backcountry travel, or climbing—and where you can get them. As always, check with the managing agency for the most current information.

WHAT ABOUT USER FEES?

To explain the Trail-Park Pass and other user fees, and clarify where each applies, we've put together a summary, "Recreational User Fees," which you'll find on p. 7.

WHERE CAN YOU CAMP BEFORE YOUR HIKE?

Roadside camping areas that can serve as "jumping-off points" for backcountry travel are listed for each area. We've tried to indicate which campgrounds charge a fee (with the $ symbol), but please note that these fee listings are not complete. You'll find information on how to reserve individual or group sites where available. Campgrounds may be closed due to road closures, budgetary constraints, or other conditions. Call the managing agency for current information.

Many national forest campgrounds are first-come, first-served, but reservations are available at approximately half of them by calling (800) 280-CAMP (at these areas 60% of the sites are reservable); a small fee is charged (a brochure with details, "Reservations in National Forest Recreation Sites," is available from ranger districts and Forest Service headquarters). You can also call this number to get information on which campgrounds are reservable, as this list seems to be constantly changing. No-fee campgrounds are nonreservable. There are no reservable individual sites at National Park Service campgrounds in Washington, Oregon, or Idaho (there are a few reservable group campgrounds—call the appropriate park for information).

WHAT ABOUT MAPS?

We have chosen not to list the individual topographical maps covering the various wilderness areas (with the exception of specialized National Park Service topo maps covering the whole of each park). A list of maps, by itself, is not especially useful. You'll need a guidebook to determine what areas and trails to cover, and once you've done that, you can choose from a number of different sources of excellent topographic maps covering Washington's mountains and backcountry. Most are available at map stores, backpacking and camping stores, ranger stations, park, and forest information centers, and The Mountaineers bookstore—or they can be ordered directly from the publisher.

USGS topographic maps are excellent for delineating fairly small topographic details and so are essential for off-trail, cross-country exploration. Revision is done infrequently though, and road and trail information may be very outdated. Contact the United States Geological Survey (USGS) Information Services at Box 25286, Denver, CO 80225, (800) USA-MAPS.

The **Green Trails**™ series, which covers most hiking areas in the Cascades and Olympics, and the **Custom Correct**™ series, covering the Olympics, are made from data "separations" purchased from the USGS. These two commercial publishers have kept their maps up to date, added and deleted information, and issued maps specifically designed for hikers. Contact Green Trails at P.O. Box 77734, Seattle, WA 98177, (800) 762-6277. Contact Custom Correct at Little River Enterprises, 3492 Little River Road, Port Angeles, WA 98363; (360) 457-5667.

Trails Illustrated™ publishes rainproof topo maps covering entire national parks. For Washington these include Mt. Rainier National Park, North Cascades National Park, and Olympic National Park. Contact them at Trails Illustrated, P.O. Box 3610, Evergreen, CO 80439, (800) 962-1643.

The **USFS** publishes topographic maps for many wilderness areas under its management and also offers non-topographic recreation maps covering each of the national forests in Washington. These recreation maps are excellent for finding roads and locating general landmarks and most trails. Contact the National Forest headquarters—ranger stations will have maps of local interest on hand for purchase. Forest Service maps use the USGS topographical base, but include all road and trail numbers.

The **National Park Service** publishes a brochure for each area it administers. These are general interest maps that are useful for travel on roads and for locating general landmarks and most trails (more detailed topo maps should be used for backcountry travel).

Recreational User Fee Demo Projects In Washington

New user fees are now in effect in many of this region's National Forests, Parks, and Monuments (and at many non-wilderness locations not included in this book). These fees may be in addition to fees (such as entrance or campground fees) that are already col lected. This program was passed in response to dwindling agency budgets and a growing backlog of trail maintenance needs, and at least 80% of any new revenues collected under this pilot project will remain with the area where they are collected to fund local trailhead and trail maintenance projects.

Because this is a demonstration project (the law expires in 1999), agency experimentation with different types of recreation fee systems has been strongly encouraged and, as a result, a number of different fee programs have been instituted here in Washington. Fortunately, most National Forest trailheads in Washington and Oregon are covered by a region-wide trailhead parking fee, the Trail-Park Pass, modeled after the Sno-Park system used in winter. You'll find a summary of these fees below.

THE TRAIL-PARK PASS

The Trail-Park Program has been adopted so far by the Columbia Gorge National Scenic Area, Deschutes, Gifford Pinchot, Mt. Baker–Snoqualmie, Mt. Hood, Okanogan, Olympic, Rogue River, Siskiyou, Suislaw, Umatilla, Wallowa–Whitman, Wenatchee, and Willamette National Forests. The Trail-Park Pass is required for parking within 1/4 mile of trailheads. Fees are $3 per car per day and $25 for an annual pass. The annual pass is transferable between two vehicles—a family pass of $5/year (in addition to the $25) allows use of both vehicles at the same time. Passes are not available for purchase at trailheads. Plan to purchase your pass prior to arriving at the trailhead (see "Where Do I Buy One?" below).

Mt. Baker–Snoqualmie National Forest ....**(425) 775-9702**

Trail-Park Pass required at most trailheads.

Heather Meadows area requires a separate parking permit—$5/vehicle/3 days, $15/season (the Forest Service will accept *annual* Trail-Park Passes for parking at Heather Meadows).

Olympic National Forest ....**(360) 765-2200**

Trail-Park Pass required at most trailheads.

Wenatchee National Forest . ...**(509) 662-4335**

Trail-Park Pass is required at most trailheads.

Dispersed camping fee in South Fork Tieton area, $5/vehicle/night. Trail-Park Pass will be honored at trailheads.

Dispersed camping fee in Chiwawa drainage, $4/vehicle. Trail-Park Pass will be honored at trailheads.

Okanogan National Forest . ...**(509) 826-3275**

Trail-Park or Okanogan Pass required for *overnight* parking at trailheads (some changes may occur before summer 1998; contact ranger district for final details). Okanogan Pass required for dispersed and campground overnight use west of the Okanogan River—$5/night, $10/3 nights, $25/season. No additional fees will be charged at established campgrounds.

Trail-Park Pass can be used only at Forest Service trailheads.

Gifford Pinchot National Forest . . . .**(360) 891-5000**

A Monument Pass is required for designated developed sites within the Mount St. Helens National Volcanic Monument (which include the visitor center complexes, viewpoints, and interpretive sites)—$8/3 days, $16/year, children 15 and under free.

Permit required for any climbing above 4,800 feet on Mount St. Helens—$15/person/day, $30/year (fee charged April 1–October 31). Subject to availability.

Mount Margaret Backcountry use fee starting in 1998—$10/site/night.

Trail-Park Pass required at most trailheads outside National Volcanic Monument.

Olympic National Park . . . .**(360) 452-0330**

Entrance fees (charged only at existing entrances)—$10/vehicle/7 days, $5/person/7 days, $20/year (at Olympic National Park only).

Backcountry Overnight Use fees—$5/permit plus $2/person per night; maximum fee for group of 6 is $50, maximum fee for group of 12 is $100; Frequent User Pass (issued to individuals) covers backcountry overnight use fees and costs $30/year ($15/year for a member of the same household).

Ozette parking fee will be charged in addition to backcountry use fees (if any)—$1/vehicle per day. Frequent User Pass (described above) can be used to cover this fee requirement.

Higher camping fees at larger campgrounds with more services within the Park, including Sol Duc Hot Springs.

Mount Rainier National Park . . . .**(360) 569-2211**

Entrance fees (charged only at existing entrances)—$10/vehicle for 7 days, $5/individual for 7 days, $20/year (at Mt. Rainier National Park only).

Columbia Gorge National Scenic Area . . . .**(541) 386-2333**

Trail-Park Pass to be required at most trailheads.

DISCOUNTS?

Golden Age/Access passports generally entitle holders to half-price Forest Service permits.

Participants in organized volunteer work on Forest Service lands are eligible for free Trail-Park Passes. A trails volunteer receives a volunteer day pass for each day of trail work performed. Volunteers can trade two such day passes for an annual volunteer Trail-Park Pass, even if the day passes were acquired during the previous calendar year. For more information or a list of organized trail work activities, contact your local Forest Service office or the Volunteer Trailwork Coalition at (206) 464-1641.

Golden Eagle passes will cover entrance fees only at Department of Interior sites—$50 per year.

WHERE DO I BUY ONE?

Forest Service permits will be sold through Forest Service and National Park Service offices, visitor centers (including the Outdoor Recreation Information Center (ORIC) at REI's flagship store in Seattle, (206) 470-4060, and a growing list of private vendors, including The Mountaineers clubhouse bookstore, (206) 284-6310 (the Nature of the Northwest Web site at http://www.naturenw.org/forest/tpvendor.html has a listing of some of the private vendors). They are also increasingly available by mail, phone, and online, including from National Forest Headquarters (make checks payable to "USDA-Forest Service"), NWIA Headquarters in Seattle (206) 220-4140, with a valid credit card), and WTA online, http://www.wta.org/wta/.

Park Service permits available at Park Service visitor centers and entrance stations.

Backcountry Camping and Travel

A NOTE ON WILDERNESS

The wild places that remain on Earth hold a special value for each of us. Wilderness is a place where we can temporarily escape the pressures of modern life and get in touch with our more primal selves—communing with nature and reflecting in the silence, solitude, majesty, and wonder. Wilderness is defined in the Wilderness Act of 1964 as "an area where the earth and its community of life are untrammeled by man, where man himself is a visitor who does not remain." Wilderness is a particularly fragile treasure, with limited abilities to accommodate the intrusions of man. "[T]o cherish we must see and fondle," warned Aldo Leopold, "and when enough have seen and fondled, there is no wilderness left to cherish."

Can we both enjoy and protect these diminishing islands of wildness—leaving them untrammeled enough that future generations can experience the same wonderment and revitalization as we do? Nature knows no unchanging wilderness, and the natural environment undergoes constant evolution whether man is present or not. The key is to minimize the influence of man in that change.

With more people than ever now descending on the backcountry, some rules and regulations are necessary to protect and preserve its basic integrity. But rules and regulations, without an abiding respect for these wild places and their inhabitants, are not enough to keep our favorite wilderness haunts from being loved to death. We must each take responsibility to educate ourselves and become equipped with the skills and habits that enable us to Leave No Trace (see "Wilderness Ethics/Leave No Trace" on p. 13).

The rules and regulations that apply to designated wilderness are more restrictive than those applying to the national forest lands within whose boundaries they usually lie. But the principles and practices of leaving no trace should guide our actions in all wild places, designated wilderness or not. While most of the areas covered in this *Access Guide* are designated wilderness areas, many unprotected, pristine, roadless areas (unfortunately fewer every year) remain in our national forests and on state land (see a partial list on p. 12). We encourage you to explore these areas and urge you to treat all wild places with care and respect, so they can remain relatively untrammeled for generations to come. Monitor their health, lobby for their protection, and tread lightly on the land wherever you go.

WTA Trails Report Web Site
http://www.wta.org/wta/

The Washington Trail Association Web site features a complete database of all U.S. Forest Service and National Park Service trails in Washington State. In addition, visitors to the site are encouraged to leave reports of their trail experiences. These reports are then cross-referenced with the trail database to create a trail "guide" service complete with current conditions. There is also information on WTA's trail maintenance program, including a listing of upcoming work parties and directions on how to volunteer.

AN OVERVIEW OF RULES AND REGULATIONS

What follows are general regulations and guidelines that apply to the wilderness areas, national forests, and national parks in Washington. Familiarize yourself with this information first and then refer to the particular areas you intend to visit for information and regulations specific to those places. While we've tried to be as comprehensive and current as possible, contacting the agency managing a particular area is still the best way to get the most up-to-date information. You'll find a list of the appropriate managing agencies to contact under each wilderness area and National Park and Monument, and a complete listing of all National Forest ranger districts and headquarters addresses and phone numbers on pp. 92–95.

- **Party size is limited** in Washington wilderness areas (as well as national parks). The allowed group size varies, but is always twelve people or less.[1]
- **Motorized vehicles and equipment** are prohibited in wilderness areas.
- **Bicycles and hang gliders** are prohibited in wilderness areas (see "Knobby Rules" on p. 12 for more complete mountain bike access information) as are wagons, carts, and other wheeled vehicles.[2] Mountain bikes are also not allowed on National Park trails[3] or on the Pacific Crest Trail.
- **Shortcutting trail switchbacks** is prohibited in National Parks, National Forests, and wilderness areas. This practice damages the trail, soil, and vegetation.
- **Campfires** are often prohibited above certain elevations and in other specific areas within most wilderness areas.[4] Campfires may also be prohibited due to fire danger, inadequate firewood sources, and other ecological concerns. Check with ranger districts for wilderness and national forest and park closure areas. In all subalpine areas, above treeline, or above 4,000 feet, even in areas where campfires are otherwise allowed, stoves are strongly suggested (and fires discouraged) due to the fragile ecosystem and lack of firewood. Use of portable stoves, as a general practice in all wilderness areas, is now strongly encouraged.

---

[1] All wildernesses within Gifford Pinchot, Wenatchee, and Mt. Baker–Snoqualmie National Forests have a party size limit of 12 (people plus stock). In the Lake Chelan-Sawtooth and Pasayten Wilderness (and Wenaha-Tucannon and Oregon wildernesses within Umatilla NF) groups may consist of no more than 12 persons or more than 18 pack and saddle animals. In the five wildernesses of Olympic NF and Olympic NP the limits are 12 persons and/or 8 head of livestock. Lower limits may exist in certain National Park off-trail areas.

[2] Mobility-impaired individuals in wheelchairs are exempt, but their wheelchairs must conform to certain restrictions under ADA.

[3] Olympic NP has two exceptions—the old Boulder Creek Road up about 2 miles to the "old" parking lot, 1/4 mile before the hot springs, and the Spruce Railroad Trail at Lake Crescent.

[4] In the Alpine Lakes Wilderness, campfires are prohibited above 4,000 feet on the west side of the Cascades and above 5,000 feet on the east side; above 3,500 feet in the Olympic NF wildernesses and in Olympic NP west of the Elwha River and the North Fork of the Quinault River (above 4,000 feet in the rest of the Park east of these rivers); and in Mt. Rainier NP (except in fireplaces in roadside campgrounds).

- **Cutting or defacing standing trees,** dead or alive, including snags and boughs, is not permitted. Healthy trees and decrepit snags are important components of the ecosystem, are needed by wildlife, and are beautiful.
- **Restoration/Rehabilitation:** Being in an area posted as closed for restoration, revegetation, or rehabilitation is prohibited. Do not walk on or camp in these areas.
- **Caching,** leaving, or storing equipment, personal property, or supplies unattended for more than 48 hours is not allowed in Cascade Range wilderness areas (24 hours in wildernesses of Olympic NF, 72 hours in Umatilla NF). Caching is prohibited in Olympic NP, North Cascades NP, and Mt. Rainier NP (except at a few specific locations at Rainier for Wonderland Trail hikers).
- **Many trails and some wildernesses are closed to stock.** Where stock is permitted, pack and saddle animals are to be kept at least 200 feet from lakes, not grazed, hitched, tethered, or hobbled within 200 feet of lakes, and not tethered to trees or other vegetation (except for incidental use of very short duration). The use of high-lines, hobbles, and/or moveable pickets helps prevent damage to trees and other vegetation. **Unprocessed hay, grain, or other forms of livestock feed** are prohibited (any feed that may serve as a seed source for non-native plants, noxious weeds, or other undesirable plants is considered unprocessed). See "Use Horse Sense in the Backcountry" on p. 30 for full details.
- **Air dropping** supplies or people in wilderness areas is prohibited. Landing of aircraft is also not allowed.
- **Disturbing and collecting artifacts,** such as Native American arrowheads or rock art panels, is prohibited by law.

SOME OTHER IMPORTANT REGULATIONS AND CONSIDERATIONS

- **Camping within 100 feet** of the shoreline of any lake is discouraged. Several wildernesses do have specific prohibitions on camping within 100 or 200 feet of lakes. Check the regulations of individual wilderness areas for details.
- **Hunting** is allowed in all national forest wildernesses and national recreation areas with a Washington State hunting license. Hunting and firearms are prohibited in national parks. Firing a gun in national forests and national recreation areas is not allowed in or within 150 yards of a residence, building, campsite, developed recreation site, or occupied area; or across or on a road, or across a trail or body of water. Refer to Washington State Hunting Regulations.
- **Fishing** is usually permitted, with a Washington State fishing license, unless it affects designated Critical Habitat for a sensitive, threatened, or endangered species. No license is generally needed in Mt. Rainier NP or high lakes in Olympic NP—refer to each park's regulations for the exceptions.
- **Dogs** are prohibited on national park trails,[5] but are allowed on a leash in national recreation areas (don't need to be on a leash in Mt. Baker NRA). Dogs are allowed on national forest trails with the exception of the Enchantment Permit Area and Table Mountain Trail. On some trails in the Alpine Lakes Wilderness they must be on a leash and they must be under voice control or leash at all times in other areas.
- **Practice "Leave No Trace" camping** (see "Wilderness Ethics/Leave No Trace" on p. 13) and leave the backcountry cleaner than you found it. Among the most important suggestions: **Protect water quality.** All washing should be done well away from

---

[5] Exceptions: Seeing eye dogs. Olympic NP does allow dogs on a leash from Rialto Beach to Hole in the Wall and on the Kalaloch beaches. Dogs are permitted on the Pacific Crest Trail, but must be under physical restraint at all times while in a National Park.

any water source. Never wash your hands or dishes, or use soap (even "biodegradable"), in a lake or stream. **Bury human waste** away from water sources. Select a site at least 100 feet from water whenever possible. Bury your waste in a hole 4–6 inches deep and cover with dirt. Use backcountry toilets when available. Pack out toilet paper. **Pack out all litter.** Aluminum (including foil-lined packets and gum wrappers) and glass do not burn. Do not put refuse into a backcountry toilet or bury it—animals and frost heave can dig it up.

UNDESIGNATED WILDERNESS AND BACKCOUNTRY AREAS

Many pristine lands worthy of wilderness protection remain outside the official protection of the Wilderness Act. These are areas whose character could (and in many cases should) have merited inclusion as designated wilderness. They offer trails, solitude, beauty, and adventure, and provide vital habitat for fish and wildlife. Treat them as you would any wilderness and find ways to speak up for their protection. Below is a list of some of this state's more noteworthy areas containing significant tracts of roadless lands.

In Western Washington:

North Fork Nooksack River
Baker Lake Basin
Mountain Loop Highway
North Fork Skykomish River
Middle Fork Snoqualmie River
Greenwater (north of Mt. Rainier)
Lena Lake (eastern Olympics)
Mt. Muller (Olympic Peninsula, between Strait and Olympics)
Klickitat Trail (south of Packwood and east of Randle)

In Eastern Washington:

North Fork Entiat River
North Fork Teanaway River
Upper Methow/Mt. Ballard/Golden Horn/PCT (between Hart's Pass and North Cascades Highway)
Tiffany (northwest of Conconully and northeast of Winthrop)

Knobby Rules

(The Mountain Biker's Emily Post)

No bicycles are allowed in any Wilderness Area, as stipulated in the Wilderness Act of 1964: "There shall be no form of mechanical transport . . . in any such area." Mountain bikes are also not allowed on trails in national parks; only old roads and abandoned railroad grades are open for riding in these areas. Mountain bikes are not allowed on "Hiker Only" trails, which generally receive this designation because they are either too short, too crowded, or too boggy for riding. The entire Pacific Crest National Scenic Trail is closed to mountain bikes from Mexico to Canada. The final restrictions to watch out for are seasonal closures on certain roads and trails. When the Forest Service gates or closes a road, mountain bikes are welcome. When the county or private landowners close a road, get permission before entering the area. Seasonal closures on trails usually apply to mountain bikes, as the wheels may cause ruts in soft, wet ground.

From Tom Kirkendall, *Mountain Bike Adventures in Washington's North Cascades and Olympics.* 2nd ed. The Mountaineers, 1996.

Wilderness Ethics/Leave No Trace

Each of us who visits the wilderness has a responsibility to future generations to treat these areas in a manner that preserves their wild character. It's much more a matter of attitude and respect than of rules and regulations. As the pressures on the land continue to increase, it becomes essential that responsible users exercise an ever greater stewardship of this irreplaceable resource. You should be prepared to travel lightly on the land and to leave no trace of your visit. As the number of people using the backcountry wilderness for recreation continues to grow, the little things we each do add up and cause real impacts.

The National Park Service, the Forest Service, and other federal land management agencies, along with the National Outdoor Leadership School (NOLS) have developed **Leave No Trace,** a national educational program of minimum impact guidelines (http://www.lnt.org). The Mountaineers have refined these guidelines into easily remembered principles.

LIMIT THE SIZE OF YOUR PARTY.

The maximum party size is twelve (twelve beating hearts when counting pack-stock) in almost all wilderness areas. In many fragile areas it is even less to reduce the environmental impacts and to preserve solitude for visitors. Always check on the appropriate limits with the responsible agency when planning a trip.

STAY ON ESTABLISHED TRAILS. DO NOT CUT SWITCHBACKS.

Cutting switchbacks causes erosion and damages the trail, the soil, and vegetation. Minimize impact at a campsite. Stay on established trails around camps and avoid making new social trails. Wear soft-soled shoes around camp.

When traveling cross-country tread lightly to minimize damage to vegetation and soil slopes. When in a group, spread out rather than walk single file, to avoid creating new trails and impacting plant life. Go beyond the suggestion: "Take only pictures; leave only footprints." Heather and huckleberry, and plants just getting a foothold, break easily when stepped on. Walk on snow or rock where possible.

CAMP IN ESTABLISHED CAMPSITES WHENEVER AVAILABLE. DO NOT CAMP ON HEATHER OR FRAGILE MEADOWS.

Camp on established, unvegetated campsites rather than creating new sites and destroying fragile plants and grasses. When away from established campsites, look for previously used sites or rocks or snow to camp on. Don't trench around your tent, but carefully site it where good drainage will keep you dry. Locate your camp at least 200 feet from a lake or stream, if possible. Plants along the shore are easily trampled and killed by tents and packs. Respect other visitors' desire for solitude. Keep noise down, so that others may experience solitude. Camp in sheltered areas, away from trails and water.

PROPERLY DISPOSE OF HUMAN WASTE AWAY FROM WATER, TRAILS, AND CAMPSITES.

Urinate on rocks to avoid animals scraping delicate surfaces to get to the minerals left behind. Use backcountry composting toilets where available and don't put anything but your own waste into them. Where toilets are not available, bury all human waste in a cat hole, 4–6 inches deep, dug at least 100 feet from water and away from camp. Retain the soil plug and replace it when finished. Microbiotic activity is greatest in the layer of soil just below the surface. Pack out toilet paper; don't burn it or bury it in ground or snow— animals or snowmelt may uncover it. In high alpine areas (above treeline) and on snow or glaciers consider bagging human feces and packing it out.

USE A STOVE INSTEAD OF BUILDING A FIRE WHENEVER POSSIBLE.

Always bring a backpacking stove to cut down on impacts to fragile lands, even in areas where campfires are allowed. At higher elevations it is essential to use a stove—firewood is scarce and campfires leave obvious signs of human activity. Campfires are usually prohibited in these alpine zones. If a fire is absolutely necessary, build it in a safe spot where there is already a fire ring or fires have been built before. Keep it small. Use dead and downed wood only; never cut living trees or dead snags, which form useful habitat for animals. Before breaking camp, douse fires completely with water and scatter the cold ashes. Spread needles and twigs over the fire scar. Some wilderness users also suggest making a fire on a "space blanket" to avoid scorching the earth, although reports on effectiveness of commercial space blankets are mixed.

PROTECT WATER QUALITY. WASH WELL AWAY FROM CAMPS AND WATER SOURCES.

Properly dispose of waste water; avoid the use of non-biodegradable soap. Do not wash your dishes or yourself in streams or lakes, even with biodegradable soap (it's fine to swim, but never use soap near lakes or streams). Carry water for washing at least 100 feet away from the stream or lake. Remove food scraps before washing. Dump waste water into a cat hole in well-drained soil or fling it in a wide arc so the small drops can evaporate quickly.

LEAVE FLOWERS, ROCKS, AND OTHER NATURAL FEATURES UNDISTURBED. KEEP WILDLIFE HEALTHY AND SELF-RELIANT BY NOT FEEDING THEM.

Pack out all uneaten food. Store food in well-sealed containers, suspended from tree branches at least 12 feet above the ground and 10 feet away from the trunk, to keep it safe from animals, especially bears. Hanging food bags from trail bridges or over cliffs is also a good technique. Consider using bearproof containers (which also provide rodent protection). Consider leaving your dogs at home. Dogs disturb wildlife—even when not chasing them, dogs leave scents that drive wildlife out of an area or disrupt their feeding habits. (In addition, dogs may detract from other campers' wilderness experience.)

PACK OUT ALL PARTY LITTER PLUS A SHARE OF THAT LEFT BY OTHERS.

Pack out your garbage, including used toilet paper. Do not bury waste; animals dig up garbage pits and scatter the trash. Aluminum cans and foil will not burn. Don't leave them in fire rings. Cigarette butts and pull tabs are litter. Twist ties, small pieces of foil and cellophane, and candy bar wrappers fall out of pockets. Pick them up and pack them out.

MINIMIZE THE NUMBER OF PACK ANIMALS.

When you're using pack animals, minimize the number of stock you use by cutting down on what you pack in. Keep animals away from water (except to drink) and tether them using a highline, hobble, or moveable picket. Limit the time they are tethered to avoid damaging ground and trees. Don't let them paw at roots around trees. Scatter all manure before breaking camp. (For more details on pack stock management in the backcountry, see "Use Horse Sense in the Backcountry" on p. 30.)

PARTICIPATE IN TRAIL MAINTENANCE WORK PARTIES.

With the growing use of backcountry trails and reduced agency budgets, the trails we hike are in increasingly bad repair. Do your part to be a good steward of the resource you enjoy: Join a group such as The Mountaineers, Washington Trails Association, or Volunteers of Washington (VOW) and contribute some sweat equity toward maintaining your trails. Call the Volunteer Trail Coalition for volunteer opportunities, work parties, and training workshops, (206) 464-1641 (800) 650-1641 outside the Seattle local calling area).

THE OLYMPIC PENINSULA AND SAN JUAN ISLANDS

1. Buckhorn Wilderness

Administered by the U.S. Forest Service

LOCATION: In Jefferson and Clallam Counties southeast of Sequim, north of the Dosewallips River, bordering on Olympic National Park.

GENERAL DESCRIPTION: Located in the northeastern corner of Olympic National Forest, the 44,258-acre Buckhorn Wilderness lies on either side of the Dungeness River, which drains along a glaciated valley to the Strait of Juan de Fuca. Several other rivers and creeks drain from rocky, 7,000-foot peaks to forested lowlands, offering good entry points to the high country for hikers and climbers. The southern section has many peaks of varying difficulty that lure climbers.

GETTING THERE: From the north and east, take US Highway 101 to Forest Roads 27, 28, 2610, 2740, 2750, 2760, 2820, 2860, 2870, and 2880, then trailheads. Also accessible from Olympic National Park via the Gray Wolf, Royal Basin, Dosewallips, and Constance trails.

NEW IN '98: Trail-Park Pass required to park at trailheads (see "User Fee" summary on p. 7).

REGULATIONS AT A GLANCE

User fee . . . . .Yes*
Overnight backcountry use permit required . . . . .No
Day use permit required . . . . .No
Party size limit (people) 12
Party size limit (stock) 8

*Trail-Park Pass required to park at trailheads (see "User Fee" summary on p. 7).

ROADSIDE CAMPGROUNDS: Elkhorn (18 sites, $), Dosewallips (32 tent-only sites, $, in Olympic NP). A group camp is available in Sequim Bay State Park (100-person capacity). Contact the state park to reserve, (360) 683-4235. This state park is off US Highway 101.

NEAREST SERVICES: Sequim, on the north, and Quilcene, on the southeast, have gas, food, and lodging.

RANGER DISTRICTS

* Olympic National Forest, **Quilcene Ranger District** (address/phone on p. 94)
* **Hood Canal Ranger District** (USFS/NPS/WA State Parks) (address/phone on p. 94)
* National Park Service, **Dosewallips Ranger Station** (summer only), Brinnon (address on p. 24)

Information, trip planning, books, and maps available at all three offices.

EMERGENCY CONTACTS: 911; Jefferson County Sheriff, 911; Clallam County Sheriff, (360) 417-2000; Emergency/Search and Rescue, (800) 552-0750.

REGULATIONS IN DETAIL

Permit Requirements: None required in the wilderness.

User Fee: Trail-Park Pass required to park at trailheads (see "User Fee" summary on p. 7).

Backcountry Camping: Permitted throughout the wilderness. When possible, camp at least 200 feet from lakes and trails. If crossing over into and camping in Olympic National Park, a free overnight use permit is required, available from trailheads, Hoodsport USFS/NPS visitor center, and NPS visitor centers.

Party Size: Twelve people and no more than 8 stock animals.

‣ **Special Issues:** The Mt. Townsend Trail is heavily used by day hikers. The Silver Lakes Trail is showing signs of human impact on water quality. Choose alternative routes if possible.

Restrictions: Campfires are prohibited above 3,500 feet to protect the fragile ecosystems. Gas or propane stoves are recommended. Below 3,500 feet, if a fire is necessary, use an existing fire ring and dead and downed wood only. Dogs are allowed on trails in the wilderness but not on national park trails. Stock are permitted on trails in the wilderness (but not recommended on Tunnel Creek Trail, due to steepness). Try to keep stock 200 feet from water sources. Tying stock directly to trees is prohibited, except for incidental use for up to 30 minutes. For longer periods, use a highline, hobble, or moveable picket. Processed feed is required. Caching is prohibited beyond 24 hours. If entering Olympic National Park, note restrictions on stock use (see p. 28) and be aware that campfires are prohibited above 4,000 feet, east of the Elwha River and the North Fork of the Quinault River.

2. Colonel Bob Wilderness

Administered by the U.S. Forest Service

LOCATION: Olympic Peninsula between Quinault and Humptulips rivers, Grays Harbor County.

GENERAL DESCRIPTION: This 11,961-acre wilderness sits in dense rain forest northeast of Quinault Lake and borders Olympic National Park. Steep, forested ridges running northeast to southwest converge to become one crest in the southern section and offer the main routes through the wilderness. A fire lookout, built in 1922, once sat atop 4,492-foot Colonel Bob, where views of surrounding forest lands are dramatic.

GETTING THERE: From the north, take US Highway 101 to South Shore Road, then trailheads. From the south, Highway 101 to Forest Road 22, then FR 2204 to trailhead.

NEW IN '98: Trail-Park Pass required to park at trailheads (see "User Fee" summary on p. 7).

REGULATIONS AT A GLANCE

User fee . . . . Yes*
Overnight backcountry use permit required . . . . No
Day use permit required . . . . No
Party size limit (people) 12
Party size limit (stock) 8
*Trail-Park Pass required to park at trailheads (see "User Fee" summary on p. 7).

ROADSIDE CAMPGROUNDS: There are no campgrounds at wilderness trailheads. The nearest campground is Campbell Tree Grove on the Humptulips River (8 tent/3 RV sites). Farther west are the Falls Creek USFS Campground (28 tent/3 RV sites, $) and Willaby USFS Campground (22 tent/RV sites, $) along South Shore Road at Quinault Lake, near the Quinault USFS Ranger Station. Expect limited primitive camping in the wilderness near the few water sources. Bring plenty of water. There is an NPS-run group camp available about 30 miles away at Kalaloch (30-person capacity, $). Reserve by calling Kalaloch Information Station (see p. 23). Ocean City State Park also has a group camp (40-person capacity). Reserve by calling the state park.

NEAREST SERVICES: Lake Quinault and Amanda Park have gas, food, and lodging.

RANGER DISTRICT

❖ Olympic National Forest, **Quinault Ranger District** (address/phone on p. 94)

Information, books, and maps.

EMERGENCY CONTACTS: 911; Grays Harbor County Sheriff, 911; Information/Search and Rescue, (800) 562-8714 (24 hours).

REGULATIONS IN DETAIL

Permit Requirements: None required in the wilderness.
User Fee: Trail-Park Pass required to park at trailheads (see "User Fee" summary on p. 7).
Backcountry Camping: Permitted throughout the wilderness, but limited by thick forest and scarcity of water sources. When possible, camp at least 200 feet from trails. If crossing into and camping in Olympic National Park, a free overnight backcountry use permit is required, available from trailheads, Quinault NPS Ranger Station, Hoodsport USFS/NPS visitor center, and NPS visitor centers.
Party Size: Twelve people and no more than 8 stock animals.
Restrictions: Campfires are prohibited above 3,500 feet to protect the fragile ecosystem. Gas or propane stoves are recommended. Below 3,500 feet, if a fire is necessary, use an existing fire ring and dead and downed wood only. Dogs are allowed on all trails (though not if you cross into Olympic National Park). Stock are permitted on trails. Check with ranger station for suitability. Keep stock 200 feet from water sources. Tying stock directly to trees is prohibited, except for incidental use for up to 30 minutes. For longer periods, use a highline, hobble, or moveable picket. Processed feed is required. Caching is prohibited beyond 24 hours. If entering Olympic National Park, note restrictions on stock use (see p. 28) and be aware that campfires are also prohibited above 3,500 feet west of the Elwha River and the North Fork of the Quinault River and above 4,000 feet east of the Elwha River and the North Fork of the Quinault River.

3. Mt. Skokomish Wilderness

Administered by the U.S. Forest Service

LOCATION: East of Eldon in Mason County.

GENERAL DESCRIPTION: Protecting the headwaters of the Hamma Hamma River on the southeastern portion of Olympic National Forest, bordering Olympic National Park, this small wilderness (13,105 acres) is big on skyscraping peaks and spires and low on designated trails and traffic. Climbers and hikers who complete the strenuous climbs to the top of these 6,000-foot ridges enjoy spectacular views east to Hood Canal, Puget Sound, and the Cascades.

GETTING THERE: From the east take US Highway 101, then Forest Roads 24, 25, 2419, and 014 to trailheads. May also be accessed on the west from Olympic National Park, or by using Lake of the Angels Trail (USFS).

NEW IN '98: Trail-Park Pass required to park at trailheads (see "User Fee" summary on p. 7).

REGULATIONS AT A GLANCE

User fee . . . . Yes*
Overnight backcountry use permit required . . . . No
Day use permit required . . . . No
Party size limit (stock not permitted) 12
*Trail-Park Pass required to park at trailheads (see "User Fee" summary on p. 7).

ROADSIDE CAMPGROUNDS: Hamma Hamma (3 tent sites/12 RV sites, $), Lake Cushman State Park (81 sites, $), Lena Creek (14 sites, $), Lilliwaup Creek (13 sites), Big Creek (23 sites, $), Staircase (59 sites, $).

NEAREST SERVICES: Hoodsport has gas, food, and lodging.

RANGER DISTRICT

❖ Olympic National Forest, **Hood Canal Ranger District,** Hoodsport (address/phone on p. 94)

Information, trip planning, books, maps, exhibits, permits.

EMERGENCY CONTACTS: 911; Mason County Sheriff, 911; Shelton Police Dept., (360) 426-4441.

REGULATIONS IN DETAIL

Permit Requirements: None required in the wilderness.
User Fee: Trail-Park Pass required to park at trailheads (see "User Fee" summary on p. 7).
Backcountry Camping: Permitted throughout the wilderness. When possible, camp at least 200 feet from lakes and trails. If crossing into and camping in Olympic National Park, a free overnight use permit is required, available from trailheads, Hoodsport USFS/NPS visitor center, and NPS visitor centers.
Party Size: Twelve people.
Restrictions: Campfires are prohibited above 3,500 feet to protect fragile ecosystem. Gas or propane stoves are recommended. Below 3,500 feet, if a fire is necessary, use an existing fire ring and dead and downed wood only. Dogs are allowed on trails in wilderness but prohibited on national park trails. Stock are not permitted. Caching is prohibited beyond 24 hours. If entering Olympic National Park, note that campfires are prohibited above 4,000 feet east of the Elwha River and the North Fork of the Quinault River.

4. The Brothers Wilderness

Administered by the U.S. Forest Service

LOCATION: Jefferson County, west of Hood Canal and Brinnon, south of the Dosewallips River, bordering Olympic National Park.

GENERAL DESCRIPTION: Located in the central east side of Olympic National Forest, on either side of the Duckabush River, this 16,682-acre wilderness is steep, densely forested glacial country penetrated by only three trails. It is popular with climbers, who test themselves on Mt. Jupiter (5,701 feet) and The Brothers (6,866 feet).

GETTING THERE: From the east side take US Highway 101 to Forest Roads 25 (or 2480), 2510, or 2610, and then trailheads. May also be entered on the west from Olympic National Park using the Duckabush Trail.

NEW IN '98: Trail-Park Pass required to park at trailheads (see "User Fee" summary on p. 7).

REGULATIONS AT A GLANCE

User fee . . . . .Yes*
Overnight backcountry use permit required . . . . .No
Day use permit required . . . . .No
Party size limit (people) 12
Party size limit (stock) 8
*Trail-Park Pass required to park at trailheads (see "User Fee" summary on p. 7).

ROADSIDE CAMPGROUNDS: Lena Creek (14 sites, $), Hamma Hamma (3 tent sites/12 RV sites, $), Collins (6 tent sites/10 RV sites, $), Elkhorn (18 sites, $), Dosewallips (32 tent-only sites, $). Dosewallips State Park off Highway 101 has group campsites (maximum 128 people). Call the state park to reserve, (360) 796-4415.

NEAREST SERVICES: Brinnon, Hoodsport, and Eldon have gas, food, and lodging.

RANGER DISTRICTS

❖ Olympic National Forest, **Hood Canal Ranger District,** Hoodsport (address/phone on p. 94)

❖ Olympic National Forest, **Quilcene Ranger District** (address/phone on p. 94)

Information, trip planning, books, and maps available at both district offices.

INFORMATION CENTER

National Park Service, **Dosewallips Ranger Station** (summer only), Brinnon (address on p. 24)
Information, trip planning, books, maps.

EMERGENCY CONTACTS:

911; Jefferson County Sheriff, 911; Search and Rescue, (800) 552-0750 (24 hours).

REGULATIONS IN DETAIL

Permit Requirements: None required in the wilderness.
User Fee: Trail-Park Pass required to park at trailheads (see "User Fee" summary on p. 7).
Backcountry Camping: Permitted throughout the wilderness. When possible, camp at least 200 feet from lakes and trails. If crossing into and camping in Olympic National Park, a free overnight backcountry use permit is required, available at trailheads, Hoodsport USFS/NPS visitor center, and NPS visitor centers.
Party Size: Twelve people and no more than 8 stock animals.
Restrictions: Campfires are prohibited above 3,500 feet to protect the fragile ecosystem. Gas or propane stoves are recommended. Below 3,500 feet, use an existing fire ring

and dead and downed wood only. Stock are permitted only on the Duckabush Trail. Keep stock 200 feet from water sources. Tying stock directly to trees is prohibited, except for incidental use for up to 30 minutes. For longer periods, use a highline, hobble, or moveable picket. Processed feed is required. Caching is prohibited beyond 24 hours. If entering Olympic National Park, note restrictions on stock use (see p. 28) and be aware that campfires are prohibited above 4,000 feet east of the Elwha River and the North Fork of the Quinault River.

5. Wonder Mountain Wilderness

Administered by the U.S. Forest Service

LOCATION: In the southeast corner of Olympic National Forest, Mason County, bordering Olympic National Park.

GENERAL DESCRIPTION: At 2,349 acres Wonder Mountain is one of the smallest wildernesses in the United States. There are no trails within this wilderness, therefore it is one of the hardest to access and least used. Surrounded by an evergreen ocean of dense hemlock and fir, rocky landmarks such as Wonder Mountain (4,848 feet) lure only the hardiest climbers and cross-country backpackers with a taste for high adventure and a true wilderness experience. The headwaters of McKay Creek and Five Stream lie within the wilderness, along with several small, hidden lakes. There are no campgrounds, water, or toilets.

GETTING THERE: Take US Highway 101 on the east side of the peninsula to Forest Roads 23 and 24, then 2353, 2355, 2451, and 100 to outside wilderness boundary. (Roads are closed in fall and winter to protect wildlife.)

NEW IN '98: Trail-Park Pass required to park at trailheads (see "User Fee" summary on p. 7).

REGULATIONS AT A GLANCE

User fee . . . . .Yes*
Overnight backcountry use permit required . . . . .No
Day use permit required . . . . .No
Party size limit 12
*Trail-Park Pass required to park at trailheads (see "User Fee" summary on p. 7).

ROADSIDE CAMPGROUNDS: None.

NEAREST SERVICES: Hoodsport and Shelton have gas, food, and lodging.

RANGER DISTRICT

❖ Olympic National Forest, **Hood Canal Ranger District,** Hoodsport (address/phone on p. 94)

Information, exhibits, books, maps, interpretive program.

EMERGENCY CONTACTS: 911; Mason County Sheriff, 911; Shelton Police Dept., (360) 426-4441.

REGULATIONS IN DETAIL

Permit Requirements: None required in the wilderness.

User Fee: Trail-Park Pass required to park at trailheads (see "User Fee" summary on p. 7).

Backcountry Camping: Primitive camping permitted throughout the wilderness. When possible, camp at least 200 feet from lakes and other water sources. If crossing into and camping in Olympic National Park, a free overnight use permit is required, available from trailheads and visitor centers in the park and from the Hoodsport USFS/NPS visitor center.

Restrictions: Campfires are prohibited at lakes and above 3,500 feet to protect the fragile ecosystem. Below 3,500 feet, if a fire is necessary, use an existing fire ring and dead and downed wood only. Gas or propane stoves are recommended in this pristine area. Dogs are permitted in the wilderness, but the terrain is not suitable for stock. Caching is prohibited beyond 24 hours. If entering Olympic National Park, note that campfires are prohibited above 4,000 feet east of the Elwha River and the North Fork of the Quinault River.

6. Olympic National Park

Administered by the National Park Service

LOCATION: Olympic Peninsula in Clallam, Jefferson, Mason, and Grays Harbor Counties.

GENERAL DESCRIPTION: Situated at the heart of the Olympic Peninsula, just west of Puget Sound, the interior section of Olympic National Park includes 878,973 acres of glaciated peaks, forested river drainages, hundreds of glacial lakes, and one of the few temperate rain forests in the world. The vast majority of the park's acreage is designated wilderness, with approximately 611 miles of maintained trails leading through its wild heartland. The park is almost completely bordered by the Olympic National Forest and designated wilderness areas on the east and south sides.

Olympic National Park also includes 63 miles of Pacific coast, protected in a non-contiguous section that preserves one of the wildest and most remote shorelines in North America. Wave-pounded sandy beaches, eroded headlands, rich wetlands and tidepools, and hundreds of orphaned offshore islets make up a coastline that retains its primitive character. Cooled and drenched by Pacific storms, this maritime landscape is the home of ocean birds, fish, and seals, and the inhabitants of four Indian reservations—the Makah, the Quileute, the Ozette, and the Hoh—whose ancient traditions have endured here for thousands of years. The coastline borders the Olympic Coast National Marine Sanctuary.

GETTING THERE: US Highway 101 encircles the Olympic Peninsula, with park and forest roads leading off it to trailheads. The peninsula can be accessed from the mainland by heading west on Highway 101 from Olympia, via ferry from the Seattle area, or via the Tacoma-Narrows bridge (I-5 to Highway 16, Highway 3, Highway 104, to Highway 101). If driving from Seattle to Port Angeles, the latter route adds about 1.5 hours (driving time about 3 hours), but avoids the ferries when ferry traffic is heavy. Roads in the park that access higher elevations are subject to closure due to snow in winter. Hurricane Ridge Road is open April to October. Between October and April, snowstorms close the road on weekdays, but, weather permitting, the road is plowed and opened on weekends and holidays, closing at dusk (if there is a blizzard, the road may not open on weekends). Obstruction Point Road is closed by snow between October and early July. Deer Park Road is barricaded 2.5 miles below the ranger station in mid-October and opened again the following June. Sol Duc is usually closed by snow November through March.

Along the coast, Lake Ozette in the northern section, one of Washington's largest lakes, is at the end of a road winding south from Sekiu on the Strait of Juan de Fuca. Reach Sekiu via State Highway 112, which heads west along the coast from Port Angeles, or take US Highway 101 past Lake Crescent, then turn north at Sappho on State Route 113. Washouts and high winds can be a problem on coastal roads during winter months. Check on conditions before departure. To reach Mora on the central coast, turn west onto La Push Road from Highway 101 just north of Forks. Turn right at Mora Road at Three Rivers Junction. Highway 101 continues south and runs along the coastline from Ruby Beach to South Beach in the southern part of the coastal section.

NEW IN '98: See "User Fees" section below for full details on Backcountry Overnight Use, entrance, and Ozette parking fees.

Olympic National Park is presently developing a new wilderness plan. Programs to be implemented in the next few years (subject to funding) are a central permit system and an expanded wilderness information center. Some popular areas of the park may also be subject to new permit quotas, due to resource damage associated with heavy use. A Park Wilderness Information Center in Port Angeles is now in operation (open summers only and as staff is available at other times, (360) 452-0300).

REGULATIONS AT A GLANCE

User fee . . . . .Yes*
Overnight backcountry use permit required . . . . .Yes
Day use permit required . . . . .No
Climbing permits and cards . . . . .No
Permit fee . . . . .Yes*
Permit reservations available . . . . .Some areas
Use quotas . . . . .Some areas
Party size limit (people) 12
Party size limit (stock) 8
Dogs permitted on trails . . . . .No
Dogs permitted on beaches . . . . .Some areas
*Backcountry Overnight Use fees for backcountry camping (see "User Fees" section below).

ROADSIDE CAMPGROUNDS: Altaire (30 sites, $, shortly past Elwha CG), Deer Park (14 sites, $), Dosewallips (30 sites, $), Elwha (41 sites, $), Fairholm (88 sites, $, west end Lake Crescent), Graves Creek (30 sites, $, near end S. Fork Quinalt River Road), Heart O' the Hills (105 sites, $, shortly past Park entrance on way to Hurricane Ridge), Hoh (88 sites, $), North Fork (7 sites, end N. Fork Quinalt River Road), Queets (20 sites, $), Sol Duc (80 sites, $), Staircase (59 sites, $). All individual campsites are available on a first-come, first-served basis. No reservations taken. See Buckhorn Wilderness (p. 15), Mt. Skokomish Wilderness (p. 17), and The Brothers Wilderness (p. 18) for campgrounds outside the park on the east; and Colonel Bob Wilderness (p. 16) for campgrounds outside the park on the southwest. *Along the coast:* Kalaloch (177 sites, $), Mora (94 sites, $), Ozette (14 sites, $). Group campsites are available at Kalaloch, Mora, and Sol Duc and may be reserved by calling the ranger stations. There are no group sites at Lake Ozette.

SPECIALIZED MAPS: Trails Illustrated™ map: Olympic National Park; Custom Correct™ map sets; Green Trail™ map sets.

NEAREST SERVICES: Port Angeles and Sequim on the north side, Forks and Kalaloch on the west side, Amanda Park on the southwest side, and Brinnon and Hoodsport on the east side. Gas, food, and lodging are available, though limited, at Humptulips. Sappho has gas and food but no lodging. Limited gas, food, and lodging are available in Clallam Bay, Sekiu, and La Push, and along the coastal section of the park.

INFORMATION CENTERS

Wilderness Information Center
3002 Mt. Angeles Road
Port Angeles, WA 98362
(360) 452-0300

Backcountry information, trip planning, maps, permits, reservations.

Hours: 7:30 A.M. to 7:30 P.M. in summertime. Open as staff is available in winter.

Olympic National Park Visitor Center
3002 Mt. Angeles Road
Port Angeles, WA 98362
(360) 452-0330
(360) 452-0329 (recorded information on Hurricane Ridge weather and road conditions)

Information, exhibits, books, maps, interpretive programs.

Hours: October to May, 9:00 A.M. to 4:00 P.M.; June and September, 9:00 A.M. to 5:00 P.M.; July and August, 8:30 A.M. to 6:00 P.M. Subject to change. Call before arrival.

Hurricane Ridge Visitor Center
Hurricane Ridge, WA

Information, books, maps, summer interpretive programs, winter snowshoe tours.

Hours: 9:00 A.M. to 5:50 P.M. in summertime. In winter, hours are same as those for road opening (generally 9:00 A.M. to 4:00 P.M.)

Hoh Rain Forest Visitor Center
18113 Upper Hoh Road
Forks, WA 98331
(360) 374-6925

Information, trip planning, books, maps, exhibits, permits, summer interpretive programs.

Hours: 9:00 A.M. to 6:30 P.M. in summer. Intermittently staffed rest of the year.

Kalaloch Information Station (summer only)
156954 Highway 101
Forks, WA 98331
(360) 962-2283
(Located across from Kalaloch Lodge)

Information, trip planning, books, maps, summer interpretive programs.

RANGER STATIONS
(South Side)

Quinault Ranger Station
913 North Shore Road
Amanda Park, WA 98526
(360) 288-2444

Information, trip planning, books, maps, exhibits, limited interpretive programs.

North Fork Ranger Station (summer only; intermittently staffed)
Information, books, maps, permits.

Graves Creek Ranger Station (summer only; intermittently staffed)
Information, books, maps, permits.

RANGER STATIONS
(East Side)

Staircase Ranger Station
P.O. Box 186
Hoodsport, WA 98548
(360) 877-5569
(Located at end of Lake Cushman Road)

Information, trip planning, books, maps,
exhibits, interpretive programs.

Dosewallips Ranger Station (summer
only)
P.O. Box 197
Brinnon, WA 98320
(Located at Dosewallips trailhead)

Information, some maps, permits.

RANGER STATIONS
(North Side)

Heart O' the Hills (summer only)
876 Hurricane Ridge Road
Port Angeles, WA 98362
(Station does not receive mail)
(360) 452-2713

**Lake Crescent Ranger Station/Storm
King Information Station** (summer only)
106 Lake Crescent Road
Port Angeles, WA 98363
(360) 928-3380

Information, trip planning, maps, books,
interpretive programs.

Deer Park Ranger Station
(summer only)

Information and permits.

**Eagle (formerly Sol Duc) Ranger
Station** (summer only)
106 Lake Crescent Road
Port Angeles, WA 98363
(360) 928-3380
(Located on Sol Duc Road)

Information, trip planning, books, maps,
permits for Seven Lakes Basin.

Elwha Ranger Station
(open intermittently)
3911 Olympic Hot Springs Road
Port Angeles, WA 98363
(360) 452-9191

Information, books, maps.

In Case of Accident or for Mountain Emergencies

▲ In a *National Park*, notify the nearest park ranger.

▲ In a *National Forest*, call 911, or notify the county sheriff or forest ranger.

▲ In *British Columbia*, contact the nearest Royal Canadian Mounted Police post.

▲ If someone becomes lost or overdue, notify the nearest forest or national
park ranger, or the county sheriff.

▲ For distress or emergency, three signals or signs is the standard for alert.

▲ Before leaving for a climb or hike, always leave your plans, estimated return
time, and car license number with a responsible person.

RANGER STATIONS
(West Side/Coast)

Hoh Rain Forest Ranger Station
18113 Upper Hoh Road
Forks, WA 98331
(360) 374-6925

Information, trip planning, books, maps, permits.

Ozette Ranger Station
21261 Hoko-Ozette Road
Clallam Bay, WA 98326
(360) 963-2725 (information line)
(360) 452-0300 (Ozette backcountry reservation line)

Information, trip planning, books, maps, permits (with reservation only).

Mora Ranger Station
3283 Mora Road
Forks, WA 98331
(360) 374-5460

(Located just before Rialto Beach. Note that the road from Three Rivers Resort to the Sol Duc River bridge on Mora Road will be closed March through November 1998. Traffic to Mora will be via the Quillayute Road.)

Information, books, maps.

USFS/NPS Soleduck Ranger Station
551 S. Fork Avenue
Forks, WA 98331
(360) 374-6522

(Moved in February 1998 into Forks in the new transportation services building, on the west side of Highway 101, across from SeaFirst Bank, at the south end of town.)

Information, trip planning, exhibits, permits, books, maps.

EMERGENCY CONTACTS:

911; NPS Emergency Line, (360) 452-4501 (7:00 A.M.–midnight in summer, 7:00 A.M. –5:30 P.M. off-season); Clallam County Sheriff (north side of Park), (360) 417-2000; Jefferson County Sheriff (middle—east and west), (360) 385-3831; Mason County Sheriff (southeast side), (360) 427-9670; Grays Harbor County Sheriff (southwest side), (360) 532-3284.

REGULATIONS IN DETAIL

Use Quotas: Between Memorial Day and Labor Day, the following areas have overnight quotas in effect: Lake Constance, Flapjack Lakes, and Grand Valley. Half of the quota may be reserved no more than 30 days in advance through the Wilderness Information Center (WIC), (360) 452-0300. While no actual quotos exist for the Seven Lakes Basin (a very popular area that receives quite heavy use) there are limitations on the number of parties that may camp at specific sites—so be prepared to be flexible on where you will be able to camp. All campsites along the coast are extremely popular and fill up very quickly in summer. Between Memorial Day and Labor Day, access to the Ozette Loop is by advance reservations *only*. Check with the WIC for the most current information on quota areas.

Permit Requirements: Required for all overnight backcountry use (see "User Fees" below for specifics on the Backcountry Overnight Use fees).

Getting Permits: Permits are available from ranger stations, the Wilderness Information Center, at some trailheads, and at the Hoodsport USFS/NPS visitor center. Overnight use permits for Lake Constance, available on a first-come, first-served basis, may be obtained from the Dosewallips Ranger Station; for Flapjack Lakes from the Staircase Ranger Station; for Grand Valley from the WIC; for the Hoh River from the Hoh Ranger Station; and for Seven Lakes Basin from the WIC or the Eagle (formerly Sol Duc) Ranger Station. Permits for these areas are not available at trailheads. Half of the permits available daily may be reserved no more than 30 days in advance by calling (360) 452-0300 except for the Seven Lakes Basin for which there are no advance reservations. There is no reservation fee (user fees still apply, see below). Permits must then be picked up at ranger stations or the WIC.

Between Memorial Day and Labor Day, reservations for the Ozette Loop (between Yellow Banks and just north of Ozette River) *must* be obtained in advance (and no more than 30 days in advance). Call the Wilderness Information Center at (360) 452-0300. Successful applicants will receive a confirmation letter, which must be taken to the Wilderness Information Center or the Ozette Ranger Station and exchanged for an overnight use permit.

User Fees: Entrance fees (charged only at existing entrances)—$10/vehicle/7 days, $5/person/7 days, $20/year (at Olympic National Park only). Backcountry Overnight Use fees—$5/permit plus $2/person per night, maximum fee for group of 6 is $50, maximum fee for group of 12 is $100, Frequent User Pass (issued to individuals) covers backcountry overnight use fees and costs $30/year, $15/year for another member of the same household. Ozette parking fee will be charged in addition to backcountry use fees (if any)— $1/vehicle per day. Frequent User Pass (described above) can be used to cover this fee requirement.

Backcountry Camping: Camp only in established campsites, and on gravel bars, snow, or other unvegetated areas if traveling cross-country. Camping is permitted only in designated sites in the Seven Lakes Basin, Hoh Lake, Grand Valley, Lake Constance, and Upper Lena Lake.

Along the coast, camping is permitted on beaches, except between Ellen Creek and Rialto Beach, and on all beaches south of the Hoh River (including Kalaloch beaches). Camp on the beach above the high-tide line or use existing campsites. (Obtain copies of current tide tables from ranger stations before departure.) Use outhouses, when available. When outhouses are unavailable, dig a cat hole 4 to 6 inches deep and bury human waste at least 100 feet from any fresh-water source. Dump soap at least 100 feet from water sources.

Party Size: Twelve people and up to 8 stock animals permitted. Parties of 7–12 must use group campsites on Upper Lena Lake, Hoh River Valley, Grand Valley, and the Seven Lakes Basin Loop. No group sites are available in the Seven Lakes Basin itself (the group sites are at Deer Lake, Sol Duc Park, and Sol Duc River Trail).

▶ **Special Issues:** Wildlife in Olympic National Park is unusually accustomed to humans. Take extra care to protect food in animal-proof containers. Hang food from trees, 12 feet from ground and 10 feet away from trunk. Bear wires are available in some backcountry campsites. (See "Bear Essentials" on p. 27.)

Hikers should plan their trips along wilderness beaches with extreme care. Water adjacent to long sandy beaches can develop treacherous riptides. Surf along steep gravel beaches can cause significant undertow. Strong currents, cold water, and hidden rocks make swimming hazardous. Waves can move drift logs on the beach that can crush and kill. Be vigilant for large swells. Many creeks and rivers (Ozette, Goodman, Falls, Mosquito, etc.) can be very difficult to ford during high runoff or high-tide situations and may involve deep wading or swimming. The Hoh and Quillayute Rivers can never be crossed on foot. In addition, headland trails, marked by orange-and-black targets, lead over points that cannot be rounded by shore. They receive minimal maintenance and are usually steep and muddy. Some require climbing "sand ladders" (wooden timbers attached to cables). Be wary of loose rocks that can easily crumble or fall from above. Most important, when hiking along beaches and around coves, you must pay particular attention to tides to avoid being cut off. Pick up a current tide table and a hiking guide from ranger stations before hiking.

Bear Essentials

In bear country (which includes most of Washington's backcountry), avoid bear encounters by practicing the following:

♦ Hike in groups and make loud noises by tying bells to your backpack, talking loudly, whistling, or singing.

♦ Hike only during daylight hours.

♦ If you see a bear, walk downwind of it.

♦ Pack out everything you pack in.

♦ Keep your dog leashed, or better still leave it at home. Dogs may provoke aggression in bears and other wildlife.

♦ Keep a clean, odor-free camp, with all foods in tightly sealed, bear-proof containers.

♦ Hang food from a tree branch at least 12 feet up and 10 feet away from the trunk. Or choose an inconspicuous location at least 500 feet from camp.

♦ Cook food away from sleeping areas. Do not sleep in clothes worn while cooking.

♦ Before making camp, look for bear droppings, tracks, diggings, matted undergrowth, claw marks on trees, and nearby thick berry bushes and salmon streams that might attract bears.

♦ Never approach a bear, especially a bear cub. A protective mother is usually nearby.

♦ If charged by a bear, do not run; bears have been clocked at speeds of up to 30 mph. Movement will trigger predatory instincts in the bear. Instead, try falling to the ground and rolling into a fetal position, with your head tucked and your neck protected by your hands. Most bears become aggressive when they feel threatened and may be inclined to stop the attack if the prey appears dead.

Remember: Try to avoid an encounter with a bear at all costs.

Trail access from the north to Shi Shi Beach is closed until a new trail right-of-way can be established by the Makah Nation. Parking at this trailhead is currently a problem due to vandalism. Pay parking in an Indian parking lot may be available, but this is no guarantee of safety. Access to beaches on Indian reservations is by permission from the tribe and is at the user's own risk. The disturbance of Indian artifacts, such as rock art or structures, is prohibited on both federal and Indian lands. Current legal access to Shi Shi Beach is only from the south, starting at Lake Ozette (southern access requires fording the Ozette River and a minimum of 3 to 4 days).

Restrictions: Stock: Permitted on many park trails, but prohibited on all beaches (call the Wilderness Information Center for more information). Overnight holding corrals are available at the Hoh and Staircase ranger stations; Elwha (Whiskey Bend) also has a small corral. Hitch racks are found at the following trailheads: Dosewallips, Whiskey Bend, Sol Duc, Hoh, North Fork Quinault, and Olympic Hot Springs. Stock must be tied at least 150 feet from backcountry camps. Backcountry hitch racks are available at Olympus Ranger Station, Olympic Hot Springs, Elkhorn Ranger Station, Hayes River Ranger Station, and the Enchanted Valley. Where hitch racks are unavailable, do not tie stock directly to trees. Use a highline, hobble, or moveable picket. Processed feed is required.

Note: Stock are not permitted off maintained trails in the stoves-only zone of the park (above 3,500 feet west of the Elwha River and the North Fork of the Quinault River, and above 4,000 feet east of these rivers). Stock camping is prohibited in the stove-only zone except in designated stock camps. In addition, stock camping is limited to designated stock camps in the following areas: North Fork Skokomish (9 Stream); Duckabush River Trail (10 Mile Camp); Dosewallips (Deception Creek, Big Timber, Diamond Meadows); Hoh River (5 Mile Island, Lewis Meadows, Martin Creek); and Sol Duc River Trail (Horse Head).

Campfires: Prohibited above 3,500 feet elevation, west of the Elwha River and the North Fork of the Quinault River, and above 4,000 feet elevation east of these rivers. These are stoves-only zones. In addition, the following areas are also closed to campfires: Honeymoon Meadows to Anderson Pass, Flapjack Lakes and Gladys Divide, Sundown Lake to Sundown Pass, Elk Lake to Glacier Meadows, Three Lakes, Lakes Margaret and Mary, Martins Park, and Martins Lakes. A very limited number of campfires are allowed at Sol Duc Lake, Lower Badger Valley, and Low Divide, using designated sites with fire rings.

Campfires are permitted on ocean beaches but must be 10 feet from the nearest beach log and must be kept small. Use driftwood only. A campfire closure is presently in place on the southern section of the Ozette Loop, between Wedding Rocks and Yellow Banks and including Sand Point.

The use of stoves is encouraged throughout the park.

Caching: Prohibited, but temporary food storage is allowed. Hang food in animal-proof containers, 12 feet above ground and 10 feet from tree trunks, to deter raccoons, bears, and other animals.

Dogs: Prohibited on trails and most wilderness beaches (permitted only on Rialto Beach from Quillayute River north to Hole-in-the-Wall and the beaches at Kalaloch—must be on leash). Permitted on leash in campground. Do not leave animals in vehicles or in campgrounds unattended.

INTERNET: Olympic National Park Home Page.: http://www.nps.gov/olym/

7. San Juan Islands Wilderness

Administered by the U.S. Fish and Wildlife Service

LOCATION: In San Juan, Whatcom, Skagit, and Island Counties.

GENERAL DESCRIPTION: The wilderness encompasses 81 rocks, reefs, and islands, ranging from 0.02 acres to 140 acres in size, within the San Juan Islands National Wildlife Refuge in the northern part of Puget Sound. Uniquely the province of nesting seabirds such as double-crested and pelagic cormorants, pigeon guillemots, and glaucous-winged gulls, as well as threatened bald eagles, all the refuge islands except Matia and Turn are closed to visitors to protect nesting birds and other wildlife from being disturbed by human visitors. Boaters must remain at least 200 yards offshore of all refuge islands.

GETTING THERE: By private boat only. Some of the islands can be viewed from the Washington State ferry traveling from Anacortes to Friday Harbor and Sidney, British Columbia. Visitors to Matia Island must land at the marine state park, using mooring buoys and the boat dock (the dock is pulled from Matia Island in the winter). Boaters must remain at least 200 yards offshore. The coves around Matia Island are closed to entry to avoid wildlife disturbance.

REGULATIONS AT A GLANCE

User fee . . . . .No
Overnight backcountry use permit required . . . . .No
Day use permit required . . . . .No
Party size limit . . . . .No

CAMPGROUNDS: The only camping available is at the marine state park on Turn Island, which has a moorage, picnic tables, fire rings, and primitive toilets, and at a 5-acre area of the marine state park on Matia Island. The campgrounds are managed by Washington State Parks and Recreation (for information call (800) 223-0321). A 1-mile loop trail leads through the wilderness portion of Matia Island. Fees are charged for overnight camping.

NEAREST SERVICES: Anacortes (mainland) or Friday Harbor on San Juan Island. San Juan, Orcas, and Lopez Islands have food, gas, and lodging.

REFUGE COMPLEX HEADQUARTERS
U.S. Fish and Wildlife Service
Nisqually National Wildlife Refuge Complex
100 Brown Farm Road
Olympia, WA 98516
(360) 753-9467

Information and handouts.

EMERGENCY CONTACTS: 911; San Juan County Sheriff, (360) 378-4151; Whatcom County Sheriff, (360) 676-6650; Skagit County Sheriff, (360) 336-9450; Island County Sheriff, (360) 679-7310.

REGULATIONS IN DETAIL

Regulations pertaining to the San Juan Islands Wilderness are strictly enforced by U.S. Fish and Wildlife Service personnel. Use of the area is at the discretion of wildlife refuge managers and is subject to change, depending on wildlife status. Check with Nisqually National Wildlife Refuge Complex before departure.

Permit Requirements: None.

Backcountry Camping: Prohibited, except in designated areas of Matia and Turn Islands.

Party Size: No restriction.

Restrictions: Campfires are permitted only in fire rings provided in the marine state parks on Turn and Matia Islands. Dogs are prohibited on all islands.

Use Horse Sense in the Backcountry

Stock should be used with care to avoid damage to natural resources. Tread lightly by observing these low-impact techniques on every pack trip.

1. Obey posted party size limits. In most Washington backcountry areas, party size is a total of 12 "heartbeats." Some areas east of the Cascades are frequently used by hunters and allow more stock animals per party.

2. Unless otherwise specified, set up camps and keep stock at least 200 feet from lakes and streams, except for watering or while traveling on established trails.

3. Never tie stock directly to trees, except for short periods (less than 30 minutes) while loading and unloading. Use a highline, hobble, or moveable picket. Set up your hitch line well away from camps, trails, and streams. Make sure the animal is not allowed to paw at roots around trees. Some wilderness areas do not allow stock to be hitched overnight because of potential resource damage.

4. Hobble all grazing stock.

5. It is essential to pack in certified seed-free processed feed for stock. Unprocessed hay or feed is likely to introduce exotic species into protected wilderness areas. Feed stock processed food in the 48 hours preceding departure to ensure manure does not contain nonnative plant seeds.

6. When breaking camp, scatter horse manure, pack out your garbage, and leave your camp better than you found it.

SOME ADDITIONAL TIPS FOR YOUR PACK TRIP:

1. Check with local land managers for regulations and trail conditions that could affect your trip. Early in the season, many trails are muddy and downed logs, washouts, and missing bridges may make trails impassable to stock; other trails are too steep for stock to negotiate. Check conditions even in late summer. Many trails are very remote and receive maintenance only once a year at best. Trees can fall at any time and mid-summer thunderstorms can occasionally wreak havoc on a trail.

2. Use experienced, well-trained stock in the backcountry.

3. Bring lightweight camping gear to cut down on the number of animals needed.

The North Cascades

8. Lake Chelan–Sawtooth Wilderness

Administered by the U.S. Forest Service

LOCATION: Chelan and Okanogan Counties, on the east side of Lake Chelan, south of Washington Pass.

GENERAL DESCRIPTION: Rising abruptly to the east of Lake Chelan, the rugged Sawtooth Mountains run northwest to southeast through the 145,667-acre wilderness, which preserves the ridge line, slopes, creeks, lakes, and alpine country.

GETTING THERE: Trails leave from Stehekin at the top of Lake Chelan, accessible by floatplane or ferry from Chelan. **Note:** Ferry service is limited in winter. Call Lake Chelan Boat Company at (509) 682-2224 for schedule. Passengers may board or disembark (by prearrangement) at Prince Creek, Moore Point, and Stehekin. For schedule and information, call Chelan Airways (509) 682-5555. On the east, various forest roads from Twisp and Winthrop lead to trailheads.

NEW IN '98: Trailhead parking requirements may change. Contact Ranger Districts for latest information. See "User Fee" summary on p. 7.

REGULATIONS AT A GLANCE

User fee	Yes*
Overnight backcountry use permit required	No
Day use permit required	No
Climbing permits and cards	No
Permit fee	No
Permit reservations available	No
Use quotas	No
Party size limit (people/stock)	12/18

*Trail Park or Okanogan Pass. (See "User Fee" summary, p. 7).

ROADSIDE CAMPGROUNDS: *On FS RD 4440:* Poplar Flat (15 sites, $), War Creek (12 sites, $), South Creek (4 sites, $), Mystery Camp (4 sites, $), and Roads End (4 sites, $). Twisp River Horse Camp, *at the end of FR 4435,* has 12 sites and horse facilities, $. All are located in the Twisp River drainage on the east side of the Wilderness. There are no group camps available. See "NEW IN '98" for details on fees.

NEAREST SERVICES: Gas, food, and lodging are available at Twisp, Winthrop, and Mazama on the north and at Stehekin at lake's end. Full services are available at Chelan.

RANGER DISTRICTS

❖ Okanogan National Forest, **Methow Valley Ranger District, Winthrop Visitor Center** (address/phone on p. 93)

❖ Okanogan National Forest, **Methow Valley Ranger District, Twisp Office** (address/phone on p. 73)

❖ Wenatchee National Forest, **Chelan Ranger District** (address/phone on p. 94)

Information, trip planning, books, maps available from all three offices.

EMERGENCY CONTACTS: 911; Chelan County Sheriff, (509) 682-4578; Okanogan County Sheriff, (509) 422-3130.

REGULATIONS IN DETAIL ▰▰▰▰▰▰▰▰▰▰

Use Quotas: None. The following trails have high use and limited campsites on weekends and holidays: North Creek, Louis Lake, Williams Creek, Oval Creek and Oval Lakes, and Twisp Pass. Choose alternate routes if possible.

Permit Requirements: None required in the wilderness. If camping in adjoining Lake Chelan National Recreational Area or North Cascades National Park, overnight use permits are required (available free from NPS and NPS/USFS visitor centers in Sedro-Woolley and Glacier and from USFS offices in Winthrop, Twisp, and Chelan).

User Fee: Trail Park or Okanogan Pass (see "User Fee" summary on p.7).

Backcountry Camping: Permitted throughout the wilderness. Choose established camps where available, preferably at least 200 feet from lakes.

Party Size: Twelve people and no more than 18 stock animals.

▶ **Special Issues:** Louis Lake and West Oval Lake are heavily used and suffering human impacts on fragile natural resources. Avoid these areas if possible.

Restrictions: Stock, campfires, and dogs are permitted in the wilderness (dogs are not allowed on the Lake Chelan ferry). Use dead and downed wood only. Use existing fire rings or leave-no-trace fire techniques. Some trails may be unsuitable for stock. Check with ranger before departure. Keep stock at least 200 feet from lakes. Tying stock to trees overnight is prohibited in Lake Chelan–Sawtooth Wilderness. Use a highline, hobble, or moveable picket. Processed feed only. Caching is allowed for up to 48 hours.

9. Mt. Baker Wilderness and Mt. Baker National Recreation Area

Administered by the U.S. Forest Service

LOCATION: Surrounding Mt. Baker in central Whatcom County.

GENERAL DESCRIPTION: Situated on the western slopes of the North Cascades, the Mt. Baker Wilderness (117,900 acres) and the adjoining Mt. Baker National Recreation Area (8,600 acres) and primitive and roadless areas (45,000 acres) are popular with outdoors lovers. At the heart of the federally designated Mt. Baker Wilderness is 10,778-foot Mt. Baker itself, the third highest of Washington's ice-clad volcanic peaks and a popular climbing destination. Many trails penetrate the surrounding forests, wandering through deep drainages, up precipitous slopes, to alpine ridges with glorious views. The National Recreation Area, on the south side of the mountain, was created in 1984 in recognition of the diverse recreational activities that take place on Mt. Baker. This is a popular snowmobiling and cross-country skiing area in winter and spring.

GETTING THERE: From the south, take Interstate 5 to Bellingham, then State Highway 542 through Deming and Glacier (the highway ends at Artist Point parking lot, Heather Meadows). Several forest roads and trails leave from the highway. To reach the west side of the wilderness (closest to Mt. Baker), take Forest Road 38 from Mosquito Lake Road to trailheads. The National Recreation Area may be reached by leaving I-5 at Highway 20 and driving east through Sedro-Woolley, then north on Baker Lake Highway. FR 12, which leads to FR 13, is the only road that accesses the NRA trailhead at Schreibers Meadows.

NEW IN '98: Trail-Park Pass required to park at trailheads (see "User Fee" summary on p. 7). Heather Meadows area requires a separate parking permit—$5/vehicle/3 days, $15/season (the Forest Service will accept *annual* Trail-Park Passes for parking at Heather Meadows).

REGULATIONS AT A GLANCE

User fee . . . . Yes*
Overnight backcountry use permit required . . . . No**
Day use permit required . . . . No*
Climbing permits and cards . . . . No*
Party size limit (people and stock) 12
*Trail-Park Pass required to park at trailheads (see "User Fee" summary on p. 7 and below for information on parking at Heather Meadows).
**Voluntary registration encouraged.

ROADSIDE CAMPGROUNDS: *Off Mt. Baker Highway:* Douglas Fir (30 sites, $), Silver Fir (21 sites, $), Hannegan (5 sites); *on Baker Lake Road:* Horseshoe Cove (35 sites, $), Boulder Creek (10 sites, $), Panorama Point (16 sites, $), Park Creek (12 sites, $), Shannon Creek (20 sites, $), Kulshan (79 sites, $). **Note:** Half the sites available at pay campgrounds are reservable; half are on a first-come, first-served basis. For reservations, call (800) 283-CAMP. A fee is charged.

Excelsior Group Camp at Mile 40 on Highway 542 accommodates up to 40 people. A fee is charged. Call (800) 283-CAMP.

NEAREST SERVICES: Deming, Maple Falls, Bellingham, Sedro-Woolley, Hamilton, and Concrete have gas, food, and lodging. Glacier has food and lodging.

RANGER DISTRICTS/INFORMATION CENTERS
❖ Mt. Baker–Snoqualmie National Forest, **Mt. Baker Ranger District,** Sedro-Woolley (address/phone on p. 93) (shares with North Cascades NP Visitor Center)
❖ **Glacier Public Service Center** (summer only) (address/phone on p. 93)

Information, trip planning, exhibits, books, maps available at both offices.

EMERGENCY CONTACTS: 911; Whatcom County Sheriff, (360) 676-6650.

REGULATIONS IN DETAIL

Permit Requirements: None. Climbing permits are not required for Mt. Baker, except for very large parties using the southern approach, but voluntary registration at Sedro-Woolley, Glacier, or trailheads is strongly recommended.

User Fee: Trail-Park Pass required to park at trailheads (see "User Fee" summary on p. 7). Heather Meadows area requires a separate parking permit—$5/vehicle/3 days, $15/season (the Forest Service will accept *annual* Trail-Park Passes for parking at Heather Meadows).

Backcountry Camping: Mt. Baker Wilderness: Designated campsites must be used at Chain Lakes, and camping is prohibited within 1 mile of the junction of the Chain Lakes and Ptarmigan Ridge trails. Elsewhere, use established sites. Stoves are strongly recommended and campfires are prohibited in many locations (see details under restrictions).

National Recreation Area: Campers must camp at designated sites (identified by tent pads) in Railroad Camp (3 sites), High Camp (6 sites), Cathedral Camp (4 sites), and Mazama Park Stock Camp. No camping is allowed on the Scott Paul and Park Butte trails. Camps have mountain toilets, but may not have water. Be prepared to pack it from a distant source. Entering or camping in any area closed for restoration or rehabilitation is prohibited.

Party Size: Twelve (combined people and stock) in Mt. Baker Wilderness and no limits in NRA (groups of more than 75 must obtain a recreation event special use permit).

▸ Special Issues: This area receives high use year-round, and many trails are showing signs of human impact. "Leave No Trace" camping and hiking techniques are particularly important here. Hiking outside or on the edges of the established tread (to avoid rocks, mud, snow, or overhanging vegetation) tramples plants and contributes to erosion and widening of trails. Whenever possible, cross directly through muddy stretches and puddles to avoid creation of additional or wider paths. Shortcutting switchbacks is never appropriate and is prohibited. Maintenance of trails varies. Check on trail status with ranger station before departure. Note that the NRA, the wilderness, and North Cascades National Park all have different restrictions on use. One trail crosses into the wilderness from the NRA and two trails cross into the National Park. It is your responsibility to check current regulations with Mt. Baker Ranger District before starting out. This is bear country. Review the "Bear Essentials" on p. 27.

Restrictions: Campfires: Prohibited within 1 mile of Gold Run Pass and the following trails and destinations: Lake Ann, Heliotrope Ridge, Excelsior Pass, Welcome Pass, Low and High Divide, High Pass, Skyline Divide, Yellow Aster Butte, Ptarmigan Ridge, Winchester Mountain, Goat Mountain, Table Mountain, and Chain Lakes.

Stock: Prohibited on the Railroad Grade and Scott Paul trails in NRA and on the following trails in Mt. Baker Wilderness: Lake Ann, Boulder Ridge, Swift Creek, Table Mountain, Chain Lakes, Ptarmigan Ridge, Nooksack Cirque, Hannegan Peak, Yellow Aster Butte, Tomyhoi Lake, Winchester Mountain, High Pass, and Heliotrope Ridge. Stock are allowed only on the following trails during the indicated time periods: Excelsior, Welcome Pass, High Divide, Skyline Divide, Goat Mountain, Elbow Lake, and Ridley Creek from August 1 to November 1. Hannegan Pass from July 1 to November 1. No restricted dates for llamas, but llamas are allowed only on trails open to stock. Please check current restrictions before departure.

Dogs: Dogs are allowed on all trails in the NRA and the wilderness, except Table Mountain.

10. Noisy-Diobsud Wilderness

Administered by the U.S. Forest Service

LOCATION: East of Baker Lake in Whatcom and Skagit Counties.

GENERAL DESCRIPTION: Located on the western side of North Cascades National Park, this 14,300-acre wilderness consists of steep, forested slopes, two major drainages (the Noisy and Diobsud Creeks), alpine meadows, and peaks on the northeast. The wilderness is surrounded by 36,900 acres of primitive and roadless national forest areas and North Cascades National Park. Watson Lakes are the most popular destination in the wilderness.

GETTING THERE: State Highway 20 and Baker Lake Highway, then Forest Roads 1106 to 1107 to 11002 to trailhead. Some forest roads and trails are closed by winter snow and avalanche danger. Check before departure.

NEW IN '98: Trail-Park Pass required to park at trailheads (see "User Fee" summary on p.7).

REGULATIONS AT A GLANCE

User fee	Yes*
Overnight backcountry use permit required	No**
Day use permit required	No**
Climbing permits and cards	No**
Party size limit (people; stock prohibited)	12

*Trail-Park Pass required to park at trailheads (see "User Fee" summary on p. 7).
**Voluntary registration encouraged.

ROADSIDE CAMPGROUNDS: Shannon Creek (20 sites, $), Park Creek (12 sites, $), Panorama Point (13 sites, $), Boulder Creek (10 sites, $), Horseshoe Cove (8 tent-only, 26 tent/RV sites, $), Kulshan (40 individual sites, $). All are on County Road 11 or on Baker Lake.

NEAREST SERVICES: Concrete and Sedro-Woolley have gas, food, and lodging.

RANGER DISTRICT

❖ Mt. Baker–Snoqualmie National Forest, **Mt. Baker Ranger District** (address/phone on p. 93)

This joint NPS/USFS office offers information, trip planning, books, and maps on the North Cascades area.

EMERGENCY CONTACTS: 911; Whatcom County Sheriff, (360) 676-6650; Skagit County Sheriff, (360) 336-9450.

REGULATIONS IN DETAIL

Permit Requirements: None.

User Fee: Trail-Park Pass required to park at trailheads (see "User Fee" summary on p. 7).

Backcountry Camping: No camping within 1 mile of Watson Lakes, except at designated sites. Watson Lakes Trail is the only trail access to the wilderness. This is bear country. Please see "Bear Essentials" on p. 27.

Party Size: Twelve.

Restrictions: Campfires are prohibited within 1 mile of the Watson Lakes Trail. Hiker-only trail. Dogs are permitted.

11. Pasayten Wilderness

Administered by the U.S. Forest Service

LOCATION: Near the Canadian border, northeast of North Cascades National Park in Whatcom and Okanogan Counties.

GENERAL DESCRIPTION: This 530,000-acre wilderness includes high country on the west and high plateaus on the east, steep river canyons, dense woods, and numerous lakes. It has the largest lynx population in the lower forty-eight states and more than 600 miles of trails.

GETTING THERE: From the west, State Highway 20 to trailheads. From the east, Forest Roads 39, 53, 54, and minor forest roads to trailheads. From the Canadian border, the Pacific Crest Trail. Harts Pass Road is closed by snow every winter, usually from mid-October to July 1. A water taxi, operated by Ross Lake Resort from Memorial Day weekend through the end of October, can be used to access the northwest side of the wilderness via Ross Lake (advance reservations are advised, (206) 386-4437).

NEW IN '98: Trail-Park or Okanogan Pass required for *overnight* parking at trailheads (some changes may occur before summer 1998; contact ranger district for final details). Okanogan Pass required for dispersed and campground overnight use west of the Okanogan River—$5/night, $10/3 nights, $25/season. No additional fees will be charged at established campgrounds. (See "User Fee" summary on p. 7) Established campsites at Black Lake are limited due to restoration. First-come, first-served.

REGULATIONS AT A GLANCE

User fee . . . . Yes*
Overnight backcountry use permit required . . . . No
Day use permit required . . . . No
Climbing permits and cards . . . . No
Use quotas . . . . No
Party size limit (people) 12
Party size limit (stock) 18
*Trail Park or Okanogan Pass required to park at trailheads (see "NEW IN '98" above and "User Fee" summary on p. 7).

ROADSIDE CAMPGROUNDS: *On the west side:* Harts Pass (5 sites), Meadows (14 sites), River Bend (4 sites), and Ballard (6 sites), off FR 54. *On the east side:* North Fork Nine Mile (11 sites), Long Swamp (3 sites), off FR 38. Fourteen Mile (5 sites), DNR T-1000. *On the southeast side:* Camp 4 (5 sites), Chewuch (4 sites), Falls Creek (7 sites), off FR 51. Ruffed Grouse (4 sites), Honeymoon (6 sites), off FR 383.

NEAREST SERVICES: Twisp, Marblemount, Okanogan/Omak, Winthrop, Mazama, and Tonasket have gas, food, and lodging.

RANGER DISTRICTS

❖ Okanogan National Forest, **Methow Valley Ranger District, Winthrop Visitor Center** (address/phone on p. 93)

❖ Okanogan National Forest, **Methow Valley Ranger District, Twisp Office** (address/phone on p. 93)

Information, trip planning, maps, and books at both offices.

EMERGENCY CONTACTS: 911; Whatcom County Sheriff, (360) 676-6650; Okanogan County Sheriff, (509) 422-3130.

REGULATIONS IN DETAIL ▰▰▰▰▰▰▰▰▰▰▰▰▰▰▰▰▰

Use Quotas: None. Hidden Lakes, Black Lake, Remmel Lake, Horseshoe Basin, and Spanish Camp are heavily used and solitude is hard to find.

Permit Requirements: None at present.

User Fee: Trail-Park or Okanogan Pass required for *overnight* parking at trailheads (some changes may occur before summer 1998; contact ranger district for final details). (See "User Fee" summary on p. 7.)

Backcountry Camping: Permitted throughout the wilderness. Choose established campsites where available, preferably at least 200 feet from lakes.

Party Size: Twelve people and no more than 18 stock animals.

▶ **Special Issues:** The Pasayten Wilderness has an early deer hunting season in September in the high country.

Restrictions: Stock are permitted on most trails. Some trails may be unsuitable. Check with ranger station before departure. Keep stock at least 200 feet from lakes. Use a high-line, hobble, or moveable picket. Processed feed only. Campfires are permitted throughout the wilderness. Use an existing fire ring or leave-no-trace fire techniques and dead and downed wood only. Caching is permitted for up to 48 hours.

12. North Cascades National Park/Lake Chelan and Ross Lake National Recreation Areas

Administered by the National Park Service

LOCATION: Between Lake Chelan and the Canadian border in Whatcom, Skagit, and Chelan Counties.

GENERAL DESCRIPTION: Wild and remote, the 684,500-acre North Cascades National Park Service Complex (including adjoining Lake Chelan and Ross Lake National Recreation Areas) has some of the most dauntingly beautiful alpine scenery in the United States. The park protects a jumble of jagged peaks, glistening lakes, and more than half the glaciers in the contiguous United States and has some of the best climbing in North America. It has escaped development and is traversed by only one road: the east–west North Cascades Scenic Highway. Surrounded by adjoining wilderness areas administered by the Forest Service, 93% of the park and the national recreation areas has been set aside as the Stephen Mather Wilderness, in honor of the National Park Service's first director. The Pacific Crest Trail crosses the southern section of the park.

GETTING THERE: From the west, State Route 20 from Marblemount and from the east, SR 20 from Winthrop cross through the center of the park. Many trails leave from trailheads along SR 20. SR 20 is closed from Ross Lake to Silver Star Creek through most of the winter. State Route 542, the Mt. Baker Highway, provides access to the northwest side of the park.

A water taxi, operated by Ross Lake Resort from Memorial Day weekend through the end of October, can be used to access the northeast side of the Park via Ross Lake (advance reservations are advised, (206) 386-4437).

The Lake Chelan Boat Company (509-682-2224) operates regularly scheduled passenger-only ferries, the *Lady II* (*Lady of the Lake*) and *Lady Express*, which depart from near Chelan (or drive to Field's Point and meet them), and are used to access the town of Stehekin (at the north end of Lake Chelan) and the southern portion of the Park. You may also make arrangements to be dropped off, or picked up, anywhere along the lake. Boats daily in summer; Mon., Weds., Fri., Sun. from November 1– December 19; Mon., Weds., Fri., Sat., Sun. from December 20–March 15. Call for schedule and details.

Chelan Airways (phone (509-682-5555) offers a 30-minute floatplane ride up Lake Chelan to Stehekin.

Between mid-May and mid-October (subject to summer snowmelt), shuttle bus service is available between Stehekin (at the head of Lake Chelan) and High Bridge Campground (zone 1) and High Bridge and Park Creek (zone 2). The upper portion of the Stehekin Valley Road between Park Creek and Cottonwood is temporarily closed due to flooding by the Stehekin River and is not expected to be open for the 1998 season. A 14-seat NPS van carries visitors to both zones for $5 one-way per zone; Stehekin Adventure Company runs a 36-seat bus to High Bridge only, for $4 one-way (1997 rates). For schedules, information, or to make reservations for either service, call Golden West Visitor Center at (360) 856-5700, ext. 340 or 341, then 14. Travelers must reconfirm 2–4 days before departure.

SPECIALIZED MAPS: Trails Illustrated™ map: North Cascades National Park. USGS map: 1:100,000, North Cascades National Park.

REGULATIONS AT A GLANCE

User fee . . . . .No*
Overnight backcountry use permit required . . . . .Yes
Day use permit required . . . . .No
Climbing permits and cards . . . . .No**
Permit fee . . . . .No
Permit reservations available . . . . .No
Use quotas . . . . .Yes
Party size limit (people/stock on trails) 12
Party size limit (people/stock in cross-country areas) 6***
*Trail-Park Pass required to park at National Forest trailheads which you may be using to access National Park (see "User Fee" summary on p. 7).
**Voluntary climber registration
***See "Regulations in Detail."

ROADSIDE CAMPGROUNDS: *Off SR 20:* Goodell Creek (21 sites, $), Newhalem Creek (129 sites, $), Colonial Creek (162 sites, $). *East of Washington Pass:* Lone Fir (27 sites, USFS, $), Klipchuck, (40 sites, USFS, $), and Early Winters (12 sites, USFS, $). *North end of Ross Lake, road from Canada:* Hozomeen (122 sites). First-come, first-served. No reservations accepted. Group camps are located in Harlequin and Bridge Creek Campgrounds (on Stehekin Valley Road) and in Goodell Creek Group Campground (on SR 20). To reserve Harlequin or Bridge Creek Campgrounds, call or write to Golden West Visitor Center, Stehekin, WA 98852, (360) 856-5700, ext. 340 or 341, then 14; to reserve Goodell Creek Group Campground, call (360) 873-4590, ext. 16. Refer to Mt. Baker

Wilderness (p. 32) for information on campgrounds outside the park on the northwest, to Noisy-Diobsud Wilderness (p. 35) for campgrounds outside the park along Baker Lake, and to Glacier Peak Wilderness (p. 43), West Side, for campgrounds off Cascade River Road.

NEAREST SERVICES: Limited in the park. Gas, food, and lodging are available at Marblemount and Glacier on the west side, Mazama and Winthrop on the east, Chelan on the south, and Hope, B.C., on the north.

RANGER DISTRICTS/INFORMATION CENTERS

North Cascades National Park Headquarters

❖ **Mt. Baker–Snoqualmie National Forest, Mt. Baker Ranger District**
2105 State Route 20
Sedro-Woolley, WA 98284
(360) 856-5700, ext. 515

Park headquarters, information, exhibits, relief map, trip planning, permits, books, maps, voluntary climbing registration, and limited self-issue backcountry overnight use permits (for areas accessed via the Baker Lake Basin only).

Hours are: Memorial Day weekend–mid-October: Saturday–Thursday: 8:00 A.M. to 4:30 P.M.; Friday: 8:00 A.M. to 6:00 P.M. During the rest of the year: Monday–Friday: 8:00 A.M. to 4:30 P.M.

❖ **Wilderness Information Center (mid-May–September)**
7280 Ranger Station Road
Marblemount, WA 98267
(360) 873-4500, ext. 39

Complete backcountry information, trip planning, permits, books, maps, and voluntary climbing registration. Limited self-issue backcountry overnight use permits are available for many areas; permits for heavy-use areas are not available after hours (see "Getting Permits").

Hours are: July and August: Friday–Sunday: 7:00 A.M. to 8:00 P.M.; Monday–Thursday: 7:00 A.M. to 6:00 P.M. May, June, and September: Daily: 8:00 A.M. to 4:30 P.M. Hours are gradually extended leading up to July as more staff become available, and gradually decrease after August as fewer staff are available. Call for exact hours.

❖ **Glacier Public Service Center (summer only)**
1094 Mt. Baker Highway
Glacier, WA 98244
(360) 599-2714

Information, trip planning, books, maps, permits, and voluntary climbing registration. Self-issue backcountry permits available at 24-hour outdoor information kiosk (Copper Ridge: see "Getting Permits").

❖ **Golden West Visitor Center**
Stehekin, WA 98852
(360) 856-5700, ext. 340 or 341, then 14

Information, trip planning, permits, books, maps, exhibits, and interpretive programs. Shuttle bus service.

❖ **North Cascades Visitor Center**
Newhalem, WA 98283
(206) 386-4495, ext. 10

Information, trip planning, permits, exhibits, books, maps, and interpretive programs.

Hours: July–August: Daily: 8:30 A.M. to 6:00 P.M. September–Veterans' Day and April 15–June: Daily: hours gradually extend leading up to July as more staff become available, and gradually decrease after August as fewer staff are available. Veterans' Day–April 15: Weekends only: 9:00 A.M. to 4:30 P.M.

EMERGENCY CONTACTS: 911; Skagit County Sheriff, (360) 336-9450; Whatcom County Sheriff, (360) 384-5390; Chelan County Sheriff, (509) 682-4578.

REGULATIONS IN DETAIL

Use Quotas: Heavily used areas are Cascade Pass (Pelton Basin and Sahale Camps), Boston Basin, Monogram Lake, Thornton Lake, Copper Ridge, and the Sulphide Glacier route on Mt. Shuksan. Designated campsites in the different backcountry management zones are quickly taken on weekends during July and August. In general, limits in popular cross-country areas are 6 parties per night and designated trailside camps have 1–4 sites accommodating up to 3–6 persons in each. Be flexible in your travel plans in summer.

Permit Requirements: Required for all overnight trips into the backcountry.

Getting Permits: Free permits and most up-to-date information about trails are available at the Wilderness Information Center in Marblemount (May–September only, with self-issue permits available October–April) on day of trip or day before. For certain areas, permits may also be obtained at Park Headquarters in Sedro-Woolley, Golden West Visitor Center in Stehekin, Glacier Public Service Center in Glacier (summer only), Hozomeen Ranger Station, North Cascades Visitor Center in Newhalem, Methow Valley Visitor Center in Winthrop, and at Forest Service ranger stations in Chelan and Twisp. Limited self-issue backcountry permits are available at Sedro-Woolley (for areas accessed via the Baker Lake Basin only), Glacier, the Wilderness Information Center in Marblemount, and at Golden West Visitor Center in Stehekin. Self-issue permits are not available for heavily used areas, nor can advance reservations be made.

    Copper Ridge: self-issue permits are available at Glacier Public Service Center, but sites are designated and limited and registration with a ranger is strongly recommended. Carefully follow instructions at the kiosk for self-registering. First check availability of sites on the provided checklist, then only self-issue for a designated campsite that is listed as open for a given night, and mark the site off on the checklist. You can camp only in the designated sites for the specific nights you've selected—sites fill up and flexibility is generally not possible. **Note:** because several North Cascades trails begin in national forests, you may need a Trail-Park or Okanogan Pass to park at trailhead. Inquire at ranger stations listed when picking up your free backcountry permits (passes may be purchased at Forest Service ranger stations). (See "User Fee" summary on p. 7.)

Backcountry Camping: The park is subdivided into cross-country zones with daily limits on parties camping in each zone. Camping is permitted at designated campsites only along trail corridors and lakeshores. Cross-country travelers must camp at least 1/2 mile from trails, 1 mile from designated campsites, and 100 feet from lakes, rivers, and streams. **Note:** Many camps have been designed to accommodate a group size of 3 to 4 people. Inform rangers if your party exceeds this number, so that a larger camp can be assigned.

Party Size: 93% of the park complex is designated wilderness. The number of people allowed per group is regulated to protect wilderness values. Parties using trails and established camps have a size limit of 12 people; where stock are permitted, the limit is 12 pairs of eyes. In designated cross-country areas near Mt. Shuksan, Eldorado Peak, and Boston Basin, party size limit is also 12. The party size limit for all other cross-country areas is 6 pairs of eyes.

‣ **Special Issues:** Hozomeen Lake Trail and Camp are closed each spring to protect nesting birds.

Restrictions: Campfires: Permitted only at forested, lower-elevation camps with metal fire grates. Use dead and downed wood only. Fires are prohibited at higher elevations, due to impact of wood gathering on slow-growing vegetation. Use a portable stove.

Stock: Permitted on the following trails only: Chilliwack, Brush Creek, Big Beaver, Little Beaver, Thunder Creek, East Bank, Jack Mountain, Lightning Creek, Willow Lake, PCT, Purple Creek, Summit Trail, Rainbow Loop, Boulder Creek, Rainbow Creek, Rainbow Lake, McAlester Creek, Stehekin River, and McGregor Mountain. **Note:** Stock are allowed to travel cross-country only in certain portions of Lake Chelan NRA. Many trails in the park pass through subalpine areas that are impassable before August. Check with ranger stations for conditions before departure.

Keep stock at least 200 feet from lakeshores and streams and camp in designated stock camps with hitch rails. Use a highline strung between trees at least 8 inches in diameter if no hitch rack is available, and hobble stock to prevent damage to tree roots.

Grazing is prohibited in the National Park. It is also prohibited in the Lake Chelan NRA within 1/2 mile of McAlester or Rainbow Lakes and within 1/4 mile of Lake Juanita. Use processed feed only. Grazing is permitted on a limited basis only in Ross Lake and Lake Chelan NRAs, when forage is available and the ground is dry. A grazing permit is required, available free at the same locations as overnight back-country use permits.

Dogs: Prohibited on trails in the National Park but allowed in roadside campgrounds, if kept on a leash. Permitted on Pacific Crest Trail and in NRAs when on leash at all times.
Caching: Prohibited.

INTERNET: North Cascades National Park Home Page: http://www.nps.gov/noca/

The Glacier Peak Region

13. Boulder River Wilderness

Administered by the U.S. Forest Service

LOCATION: In Snohomish County south and west of Darrington.

GENERAL DESCRIPTION: The Boulder River Wilderness encompasses some 49,000 acres of rugged terrain in the Mt. Baker–Snoqualmie National Forest in the North Cascades. Designated in 1984, this wilderness is rough and steep, with elevations ranging from 880–6,854 feet. It contains nine small lakes and approximately 10 miles of the Boulder River in the northwestern section. In the lower drainage there is a large area of rare old-growth lowland forest. Whitehorse Mountain and Three Fingers Peak are popular climbs. The Boulder River Trail is a popular low valley walk through mossy, green forest featuring occasional big trees and beautiful waterfalls.

GETTING THERE: State Highway 530 and Mountain Loop Highway, then Forest Roads 2010, 2030, 2040, 2060, 4052, 41, 4110/4111, and trailheads. FR 2030 to Niederprum (Whitehorse) Trail has two rutted sections that require a high-clearance/4x4 vehicle.

FR 2040 to Squire Creek Trail has flood damage 1/2 mile before reaching the trailhead. Recommend parking and walking the last 1/2 mile.

NEW IN '98: Trail-Park Pass required for parking at trailheads (see "User Fee" summary on p. 7).

REGULATIONS AT A GLANCE

User fee . . . . .Yes*
Overnight backcountry use permit required . . . . .No**
Day use permit required . . . . .No**
Party size limit (stock prohibited) 12
*Trail-Park Pass required for parking at trailheads (see "User Fee" summary on p. 7).
**Voluntary registration encouraged.

ROADSIDE CAMPGROUNDS: Clear Creek (10 sites, $), Boardman Creek (2 sites), Red Bridge (14 sites, $). Turlo (19 sites, $), Verlot (26 sites, $), Gold Basin (128 sites, $). (**Note:** About 60% of the campsites at these campgrounds are reservable; call (800) 280-CAMP to reserve.) All sites are on Mountain Loop Highway, near Verlot.

Group Campgrounds: Gold Basin has 3 group sites that can accommodate up to 40 people. Other group camps are located at Beaver Creek (25 people maximum), Coal Creek (25 people maximum), Esswine (25 people maximum), Marten Creek (25 people maximum), Tulalip Mill (60 people maximum), Wiley Creek (60 people maximum). Reservations and fee for group sites are required. Call (800) 280-CAMP to reserve.

NEAREST SERVICES: Arlington to the northwest, Darrington to the northeast, Granite Falls to the south.

RANGER DISTRICT/INFORMATION CENTER

❖ Mt. Baker–Snoqualmie National Forest, **Darrington Ranger District** (address/phone on p. 93)

❖ **Verlot Public Service Center** (east of Granite Falls) (summer only) (address/phone on p. 93)

Information, trip planning, exhibits, books, maps at both offices.

EMERGENCY CONTACTS: 911; Snohomish County Sheriff, (425) 743-3400.

REGULATIONS IN DETAIL ▰▰▰▰▰▰▰▰▰▰▰▰▰▰

Permit Requirements: None.

User Fee: Trail-Park Pass required for parking at trailheads (see "User Fee" summary on p. 7).

Backcountry Camping: Permitted, except within 200 feet of Bandana Lake and Saddle Lake (Goat Flats/Three Fingers Trails). A backcountry toilet is available at Goat Flats.

Party Size: Twelve people. No stock allowed.

▶ Special Issues: The Boulder River and Goat Flats/Saddle Lake/Three Fingers Trails receive heavy use. The Three Fingers Fire Lookout is on the National Register of Historic Places. For information on what you can do to help in the upkeep of the lookout, contact the Everett Mountaineers Club/Western Washington Lookout Association at (425) 487-3461.

Restrictions: Campfires are permitted, except within 1/4 mile of Three Fingers Trail from Saddle Lake to Three Fingers Mountain and Goat Flats, and within 200 feet of Bandana Lake and Saddle Lake. Dogs are permitted, leashing is highly recommended. Stock are prohibited on all trails.

14. Glacier Peak Wilderness

Administered by the U.S. Forest Service

LOCATION: Surrounding Glacier Peak in Skagit, Snohomish, and Chelan Counties, from Cache Col (just south of Cascade Pass) to the Wenatchee River.

GENERAL DESCRIPTION: Located south of North Cascades National Park and adjacent to the Henry M. Jackson Wilderness, this 576,600-acre, remote, high-country wilderness features numerous high peaks and glaciers. The highest peak is 10,541-foot Glacier Peak, a dormant volcano popular with climbers. Elevations range from 1,100 feet (Lake Chelan south of Domke Falls) to 10,541 feet (the top of Glacier Peak).

GETTING THERE: From the west, State Highway 530 to Forest Roads 16, 20, 23, 25, 26, 27, 49, State Route 20 to Cascade River Road, and trailheads. From the south, State Highway 207 to FR 62, 63, 64, 65, 167, and trailheads. From the southeast, Entiat to paved FR 51, then improved forest roads and trailheads.

The Lake Chelan Boat Company (509-682-2224) operates regularly scheduled passenger-only ferries, the *Lady II* (*Lady of the Lake*) and *Lady Express*, which depart from near Chelan (or drive to Field's Point and meet them), and are used to access the town of Stehekin (at the north end of Lake Chelan) and the southern portion of the North Cascades NP. You may also make arrangements to be dropped off, or picked up, anywhere along the lake. Boats daily in summer; Mon., Wed., Fri., Sun. from

November 1–December 19; Mon., Wed., Fri., Sat., Sun. from December 20–March 15. Call for schedule and details.

Chelan Airways (509-682-5555) offers a 30-minute floatplane ride up Lake Chelan to Stehekin.

Between mid-May and mid-October (subject to summer snowmelt), shuttle bus service is available between Stehekin (at the head of Lake Chelan) and High Bridge Campground (zone 1) and High Bridge and Park Creek (zone 2). The upper portion of the Stehekin Valley Road between Park Creek and Cottonwood is temporarily closed due to flooding by the Stehekin River and is not expected to be open for the 1998 season. A 14-seat NPS van carries visitors to both zones for $5 one-way per zone; Stehekin Adventure Company runs a 36-seat bus to High Bridge only, for $4 one-way (1997 rates). For schedules, information, or to make reservations for either service, call Golden West Visitor Center at (360) 856-5700, ext. 340 or 341, then 14. Travelers must reconfirm 2–4 days before departure.

Shuttle bus service is also available between Lucerne and Holden Village. Cost is $6 one-way, $10 round-trip. The bus meets a boat (slow boat in summer, only boat in winter) going up-lake (at approx. 11:45 A.M.) and going down-lake (at approx. 2:30 P.M.). Must make reservations, preferably at least two weeks ahead of desired transport (also for taking bus one-way from Holden Village). Write: Registrar, Holden Village, HC 00, Stop 2, Chelan, WA 98816-9769 (no phone).

NEW IN '98: Trail-Park Pass required to park at trailheads. (See "User Fee" summary, p. 7.)

REGULATIONS AT A GLANCE

User fee . . . . Yes*
Overnight backcountry use permit required . . . . .No**
Day use permit required . . . . .No**
Climbing permits and cards . . . . .No**
Party size (people/stock on trails) 12
*Trail-Park Pass required to park at trailheads (see "User Fee" summary, p. 7).
**Voluntary registration encouraged at most trailheads.

ROADSIDE CAMPGROUNDS

West Side: These are mostly primitive campgrounds, with vault toilets and fire rings but no running water or RV dumping stations. Bedal (19 tent/RV sites, $), off FR 20; Sulphur Creek (18 sites—1 is large enough to accommodate a group, $), Downey Creek (5 tent sites on north side of road; 3 tent/RV sites near south side parking area), and Buck Creek (29 tent sites and 1 RV site, $), off FR 26; Mineral Park (6 tent sites/2 RV sites), off Cascade River Road. Tent sites (outhouse, no water) at Whitechuck Trailhead (5 sites) and at North Fork Sauk Trailhead (5 sites).

East Side: Campgrounds are reachable only by ferry or floatplane or lie along the Stehekin Road: Purple Point (15 sites), Rainbow Falls (10 sites), Harlequin Group Camp (15 sites), High Bridge (4 sites), Tumwater (27 tent sites, 41 RV sites), Dolly Varden (2 sites), Shady (2 sites), Bridge Creek Group Camp (6 sites), Lake Creek (17 sites), Park Creek (4 sites), Flat Creek (4 sites), and Cottonwood (5 sites).

Southeast Side: *Along White River:* Napeequa Crossing (5 sites), Grasshopper Meadows (5 sites), White River Falls (5 sites). *Along Chiwawa River Road:* Goose Creek (29 sites, $), Meadow Creek (4 sites), Alder Creek Horse Camp, Deep Creek (3 sites), Grouse Group

Camp, Finner (3 sites), River Bend (6 sites), Rock Creek (4 sites), Shaefer Creek (6 sites), Atkisson Flats (7 sites), Nineteenmile (4 sites), Alpine Meadows (4 sites), Phelps Creek (7 sites). *Off Lake Wenatchee:* Nason Creek (73 sites, $), Glacier View (23 sites, $), Fish Pond (3 sites). *Off Entiat River:* Fox Creek (150 sites, $), Lake Creek (17 sites, $), Silver Falls (31 sites, $), North Fork (9 sites, $), Spruce Creek (2 tent sites), Three Creek (3 tent sites), Cottonwood (25 sites, $).

NEAREST SERVICES: Darrington on the west; Granite Falls and Verlot on the southwest; Marblemount and Rockport on the north; Lake Wenatchee on the southeast; Stehekin on Lake Chelan on the east; and Holden, off FR 8301 (the latter two reachable only by boat or floatplane).

RANGER DISTRICTS/INFORMATION CENTERS

❖ Wenatchee National Forest, **Chelan Ranger District** (address/phone on p. 94)

❖ Wenatchee National Forest, **Entiat Ranger District** (address/phone on p. 94)

❖ Wenatchee National Forest, **Lake Wenatchee Ranger District,** Leavenworth (address/phone on p. 94)

❖ Mt. Baker–Snoqualmie National Forest, **Darrington Ranger District** (address/phone on p. 93)

Information, trip planning, books, and maps are available at all offices.

❖ North Cascades National Park (NPS), **Mt. Baker Ranger District** (USFS), Recreation Information Center, Sedro-Woolley (address/phone on p. 93)

Information, trip planning, exhibits, maps, books, permits.

❖ **Verlot Public Service Center** (east of Granite Falls) (summer only) (address/phone on p. 93)

EMERGENCY CONTACTS: 911; Skagit County Sheriff, (360) 336-9450; Snohomish County Sheriff, (425) 743-3400; Chelan County Sheriff, (509) 682-4578.

REGULATIONS IN DETAIL

Permit Requirements: None. Trailhead registration is requested.

User Fee: Trail-Park Pass required to park at trailheads (see "User Fee" summary on p. 7).

Backcountry Camping: As a rule, camp in wooded areas rather than in the fragile meadows and use previously used sites where available. Do not camp within 200 feet of Holden and Lyman Lakes, or within 1/4 mile of Image Lake—a designated backpackers' camp is located southeast of the lake basin and stock must camp at Lady Camp, 1 mile east of the lake. No camping with stock within Buck Creek Pass, except at designated horse camp. At Cloudy Pass, you are encouraged to camp on the basin on the east side of the Pass, rather than on Pass itself.

Party Size: Twelve (combined people and stock). Cross-country travelers should limit party size to 6.

❖ **Special Issues:** Spider Meadows, Cloudy Pass, Lyman Lakes, and Buck Creek Pass are suffering from overuse. Kennedy Hot Springs, Buck Creek Pass, White Pass, Boulder Basin and the Lime Ridge area tend to be crowded on weekends, and restrictions are in effect. Boulder Basin, a climbing camp for Glacier Peak, is an especially sensitive and overused area—it is important to stay off all vegetation. It is very difficult to hang food at the Basin and so a bearproof (marmots are the big problem) container is recommended. A backcountry toilet is provided at the Basin—when the toilet is buried in snow, visitors are asked to go below snowline and bury waste in organic soil or to bag waste and pack it out. **Note:** Schaefer Lake, White River, Little Giant, Napeequa, and Pilot Ridge Trails have river crossings that may be difficult in early season, and higher-elevation trails may be snowy until mid- to late July. The Canyon Creek Bridge at milepost 6.5 on the Suiattle River Trail will be closed for reconstruction in early spring and should be completed in summer. Fording Canyon Creek may be hazardous for hikers and will not be possible with stock. Miners Creek Bridge is impassable to stock and no ford opportunities exist at present. Remember: This is bear country—review "Bear Essentials" on p. 27 before starting out. Non-hunters may wish to avoid this area during the early season buck hunt, September 15–25. Buck Creek Pass, Spider Meadows, Boulder Creek, Suiattle Pass, and White Pass to Indian Pass are particularly crowded at this time.

Restrictions: No camping, tethering, or grazing of stock within the Buck Creek Pass areas; use designated horse camp. No stock permitted in lake basin at Image Lake—stock camp is 1 mile from the lake at Lady Camp. No camping along White Pass Ridge. Use campsites below ridge that are not under revegetation management; stoves only. Use designated campsites and fire rings within the area of Kennedy Hot Springs.

Campfires: No campfires at Ice Lakes. Prohibited within 200 feet of the shores of Holden Lake and Lyman Lake, within 1/4 mile of Image Lake and Lake Byrne, and above 4,000 feet at Lime Ridge. Stoves are strongly suggested above treeline (4,000 feet on the west side of the Wilderness, 5,000 feet on the east) due to lack of firewood and the fragile ecosystem. Use an existing fire ring and dead and downed wood only. Check with ranger districts for campfire closures before your trip.

Stock: The following trails are closed to stock: Twin Lakes, Phelps Creek Trail beyond Spider Meadows, High Pass, Upper Lyman Lake, and Lost Creek Ridge. While not prohibited, stock use is not encouraged on the Little Giant, Schaefer Lake, and White River Trails due to poor tread conditions. Downey Creek Trail #768 is not maintained for stock at this time. Kennedy Creek Bridge, leading to the PCT, is gone, so the trail is impassable to stock. Visitors need to take Kennedy Ridge Trail #639 to access PCT. Check with Darrington RD regarding Mica Lake to Milk Creek, which is currently impassable to stock. Stock are allowed only in the designated horse camp at Buck Creek Pass. Parties with stock are encouraged to use Cloudy Pass Basin horsecamp instead of Lyman Lake campgrounds (due to restoration efforts). Elsewhere, stock must be kept at least 200 feet from lakes and not tied directly to trees. Use a highline, hobble, or moveable picket. Processed feed only. Call ranger stations to get current trail conditions for stock. Due to limited trail maintenance and damage from severe storms during the winter of 1995–96, stock users should check with the appropriate ranger district prior to leaving on their trips to get up-to-date reports on downed trees, bridge problems, and washouts.

15. Henry M. Jackson Wilderness

Administered by the U.S. Forest Service

LOCATION: King, Snohomish, and Chelan Counties between Stevens Pass and North Fork Sauk River.

GENERAL DESCRIPTION: Straddling the Cascades between Stevens Pass and the North Fork Sauk River, the 103,591-acre Henry M. Jackson Wilderness contains gentle ridges, glaciated peaks of the Monte Cristo Range, and the Pacific Crest Trail (PCT). It is adjoined by Glacier Peak Wilderness on the north and 35,100 acres of semi-primitive roadless areas on the west. The Monte Cristo Range is one of the most popular climbing areas in the state. The wilderness is named for the Washington senator instrumental in legislation that created North Cascades National Park, the Pasayten and Alpine Lakes Wildernesses, and the additional areas set aside under the Washington Wilderness Act of 1984.

GETTING THERE: From the southwest, take US Highway 2, then Forest Roads 63, 65, minor forest roads, then trailheads. From the northwest, take the Mountain Loop Highway or State Highway 530 then FR 7, 20, and 49 to trailheads. From the east, take Highway 2 to FR 65, then trailheads. The PCT enters from Glacier Peak Wilderness.

NEW IN '98: Trail-Park Pass required to park at trailheads. (See "User Fee" summary, p. 7.)

REGULATIONS AT A GLANCE

User fee . . . . .Yes*
Overnight backcountry use permit required . . . . .No**
Day use permit required . . . . .No**
Party size limit (people and stock) 12
*Trail-Park Pass required to park at trailheads (see "User Fee" summary, p. 7).
**Voluntary registration encouraged.

ROADSIDE CAMPGROUNDS: *From the southwest:* Bedal (19 tent/RV sites, off FR 20, $), Troublesome Creek (6 tent-only sites, 24 tent/RV sites, off FR 63, $), San Juan (6 tent-only sites, 2 tent/RV sites, $, off FR 63), Beckler River (27 tent/RV sites, off FR 65, $). Tent sites (outhouse, no water) at North Fork Sauk Trailhead (5 sites, access to northwest corner). If heading to Monte Cristo area, see Boulder River Wilderness (p. 42) for campgrounds. *From the southeast: Off the Little Wenatchee River Road:* Theseus Creek (3 sites), Lake Creek (8 sites), Little Wenatchee Ford (3 sites), Soda Springs (5 sites). *Off White River Road:* Napeequa Crossing (5 sites), Grasshopper Meadows (5 sites), White River Falls (5 sites). *Off Lake Wenatchee:* Nason Creek (73 sites, $), Glacier View (23 sites, $), Fish Pond (3 sites).

NEAREST SERVICES: Gas, food, and lodging available at Darrington, Granite Falls, Verlot, Leavenworth, Lake Wenatchee, Gold Bar, Skykomish, and Index.

RANGER DISTRICTS/INFORMATION CENTERS
❖ Wenatchee National Forest, **Lake Wenatchee Ranger District** (address/phone on p. 94)
❖ Mt. Baker–Snoqualmie National Forest, **Darrington Ranger District** (address/phone on p. 93)

❖ Mt. Baker–Snoqualmie National Forest, **Skykomish Ranger District** (address/phone on p. 93)

Information, books, and maps are available at all offices.

❖ **Verlot Public Service Center** (east of Granite Falls) (summer only) (address/phone on p. 93)

Information, exhibits, books, maps.

EMERGENCY CONTACTS: 911; King County Sheriff, (800) 344-4080; Snohomish County Sheriff, (425) 743-3400; Chelan County Sheriff, (509) 682-4578.

REGULATIONS IN DETAIL

Permit Requirements: None.

User Fee: Trail-Park Pass required to park at trailheads (see "User Fee" summary on p. 7).

Backcountry Camping: Prohibited within 200 feet of the shoreline of Goat Lake (Goat Lake/Elliott Creek Trail). Take particular note of campfire restrictions cited below.

Party Size: Twelve (combined people and stock).

▶ **Special Issues:** Lakes in this area are heavily used, and restrictions on camping and campfires are in effect to protect natural resources from further degradation. Watch for snow until mid-July on all trails. The Goat Lake, Smithbrook, and Blanca Lake Trails receive very high use. The quiet ridges along the Cascade Crest have very little water late in the season. Non-hunters may wish to avoid this area during the early season buck hunt, September 15–25.

The Snohomish County right-of-way leading into Monte Cristo area (Silver/Twin Lakes, Glacier Basin) from Barlow Pass (Mountain Loop Highway) is unmaintained. Bridges crossing South Fork Sauk River at approximately 1 mile (Weden Creek area) and 4 miles (at entrance to Monte Cristo townsite) have collapsed. Crossing is dangerous, especially during spring run-off. Check with the Darrington RD on status.

Restrictions: Campfires are prohibited at Lake Valhalla, Glasses Lake, Heather Lake, Minotaur Lake, Theseus Lake, and Lake Sally Ann and within 1/4 mile of Goat Lake, Glacier Basin and Glacier Basin Trail, Silver Lake (Silver/Twin Lakes Trail), and Twin Lakes. Stoves are encouraged above 4,000 feet due to limited sources of wood and impacts on fragile ecosystem. Heather Lake, Minotaur Lake, and Lake Sally Ann are closed to stock (except PCT through-travel) as are the Blanca Lake, Glacier Basin, and Silver Lake Trails and the last 1.5 miles of the Goat Lake Trail. Designated hitching areas are at Lakes Valhalla and Janus. Keep stock 200 feet from lakeshores and do not tie stock to trees. Use a highline, hobble, or moveable picket. Processed feed only. Dogs are permitted on trails, but it's best to keep them leashed, especially on busy trails.

THE ALPINE LAKES REGION

16. Alpine Lakes Wilderness
Administered by the U.S. Forest Service

LOCATION: Central Cascades of King, Kittitas, and Chelan Counties between US Highway 2 on the north and Interstate 90 on the south.

GENERAL DESCRIPTION: One of western Washington's most accessible wilderness areas, 393,000-acre Alpine Lakes in the Central Cascades is also the most visited. Hundreds of miles of trails lead through forested valleys, among sharp-pinnacled peaks, to high-country lakes and tarns. There are numerous climbing destinations.

Protected since 1976 as designated wilderness, Alpine Lakes is administered by Mt. Baker–Snoqualmie National Forest west of the Cascade crest and by Wenatchee National Forest on the east side. Both forests are exploring management alternatives to balance protection of fragile natural resources with heavy weekend and summer/fall use. Visitors should expect changing regulations during the next few years. Call ranger stations for the most up-to-date information before departure.

GETTING THERE: From Seattle, either Interstate 90 to Snoqualmie Pass and south-side trailheads or Interstate 5 to US Highway 2, forest roads, and north-side trailheads. From the east side, US Highway 97 between Leavenworth and Cle Elum, then forest roads and east-side and north-side trailheads. **Note:** The Foss River Road (#68) access to Evans Lake Trail will be gated from November 1 to March 15 to protect wintering bald eagles.

Unscheduled closures may occur at any time of year due to changing road conditions. Call ranger stations for information before departure.

NEW IN '98: Enchantment Permit reservations may be made by mail and will be taken beginning March 1, 1998 by the Leavenworth RD. Call the district for an information brochure and write-in application. The Enchantment Permit fee will be $3 per person per day. Ingalls Lake and the peaks of the Stuart Range have not been added to the system for 1998. See "Getting Permits" on p. 51 for details.

REGULATIONS AT A GLANCE
User fee . . . . .Yes*
Overnight backcountry use permit required . . . . .Yes
Day use permit required . . . . .Yes
Climbing permits and cards . . . . .No
Permit fee . . . . .Yes**
Permit reservations available . . . . .Some areas
Use quotas . . . . .Some areas
Party size limit (people and stock—general) 12
Party size limit (The Enchantment Permit Zone) 8
*Trail-Park Pass required to park at trailheads (see "User Fee" summary, p. 7). See below re: Enchantment Permit fee.
** Permit fee for Enchantment, $3/person/day; other reservation areas may be subject to fee in 1998. Check with ranger districts for current information.

ROADSIDE CAMPGROUNDS

South Side: *Off Interstate 90:* Tinkham (48 sites, 60% reservable, $), Denny Creek (34 sites, 60% reservable, $). To reserve campsites, call (800) 280-CAMP. Reservation fee. Crystal Springs (25 sites, Stampede exit, $), Kachess (180 sites, 40 reservable including one group site, FR 4900, $). There are group sites at Kachess (up to 50 people, $) and Denny Creek (up to 35 people, $).

Cle Elum River Valley: Wish-Poosh (39 sites, $), Cle Elum River (35 sites, $), Red Mountain (9 sites, $), Salmon la Sac (127 sites, 26 reservable including 1 group site, $), Cayuse Horse Camp (adjacent to Salmon la Sac, 15 sites, $, horse users only), Fish Lake (15 tent-only sites, near end of Road 4330), Owhi (23 tent-only sites, beside Cooper Lake, $).

North Fork Teanaway: Beverly (16 sites).

East Side: *Off Icicle Creek Road:* Eightmile Creek (45 sites, $), Bridge Creek (6 sites, $), Johnny Creek (65 sites, $), Ida Creek (10 sites, $), Chatter Creek (9 tent-only, 3 tent/RV sites), Rock Island (22 sites, $), Blackpine Stock Camp (10 sites, $); *off Highway 2, near Leavenworth:* Tumwater (84 sites, reserve by calling (800) 280-CAMP, $), White Pine (5 sites). There are group camps at Eightmile (50–70 people, $), Bridge Creek (80–100 people, $), Chatter Creek (35–45 people, $), and Tumwater (50–70 people, $). Group campsites in the Icicle Drainage (Leavenworth Ranger District) are available only by reservation. Call (800) 274-6104.

North Side: *Off Highway 2:* Beckler River (27 tent/RV sites, some reservable, $), Miller River Group Camp (18 sites, some suitable for RVs, $), Money Creek (24 sites, some reservable, $). To reserve and for group camp, call (800) 280-CAMP.

NEAREST SERVICES: Gas, food, and lodging are available at Snoqualmie Pass and North Bend (southwest side), Cle Elum (southeast side), Leavenworth (east side), and Skykomish (north side).

RANGER DISTRICTS

Southwest Side—Snoqualmie Pass

❖ Mt. Baker–Snoqualmie National Forest, **North Bend Ranger District** (address/phone on p. 93)

❖ **Snoqualmie Pass Visitor Information Center** (address/phone on p. 93)

Northwest Side—Stevens Pass

❖ Mt. Baker–Snoqualmie National Forest, **Skykomish Ranger District** (address/phone on p. 93)

Southeast Side

❖ Wenatchee National Forest, **Cle Elum Ranger District** (address/phone on p. 94)

Northeast Side

❖ Wenatchee National Forest, **Leavenworth Ranger District** (address/phone on p. 94)

❖ Wenatchee National Forest, **Lake Wenatchee Ranger District** (address/phone on p. 94)

INFORMATION CENTERS

Wilderness Hotline: (800) 627-0062 (from Seattle local calling area 206-775-9702).

❖ Mt. Baker–Snoqualmie **National Forest Headquarters,** Mountlake Terrace (address/phone on p. 93)

❖ Wenatchee **National Forest Headquarters,** Wenatchee (address/phone on p. 94)

Outdoor Recreation Information Center (ORIC)
USFS/NPS/WA State Parks
222 Yale Avenue North
REI Store
Seattle, WA 98109-5429
(206) 470-4060

EMERGENCY CONTACTS: 911; King County Police, (800) 344-4080; Kittitas County Sheriff, (509) 962-7525; Chelan County Sheriff, (509) 682-4578.

REGULATIONS IN DETAIL

Use Quotas and Permits: Due to heavy summer/fall use, permits are required for day and overnight use of the wilderness between May 15 and October 31. In the expanded Enchantment Permit Zone (includes the Upper and Lower Enchantment Lakes Basins, Colchuck, Stuart, Snow, Nada, Eightmile and Caroline Lakes), quotas and restrictions apply, and permits are limited for overnight use between June 15 and October 15. Ingalls Lake and the peaks of the Stuart Range have not been added to the system for 1998. (See "Getting Permits" below.) Self-issued permits for all other areas of the wilderness, for both day and overnight use, are required between May 15 and October 31.

Getting Permits: Permits for day and overnight use in non-quota zones are available at ranger stations and trailheads (as are day-use permits for the Enchantment Permit Zone). Overnight permits for the expanded Enchantment Permit Zone are limited from June 15 to October 15. Enchantment Permits are only available through the Leavenworth RD. Reservations may be made by mail and reservations will be taken beginning March 1. Call the district for an information brochure and write-in application. The Enchantment Permit fee will be $3 per person per day.

A number of day-of-trip overnight quota permits for the expanded Enchantment Permit Zone (25% of total) will be available at the Leavenworth Ranger Station for those without advance reservations. A drawing will be held each morning at 7:45 A.M. Call the Leavenworth RD or the Alpine Lakes Wilderness Hotline at (800) 627-0062 for further information.

User Fee: Trail-Park Pass required to park at trailheads (see "User Fee" summary on p. 7).

Backcountry Camping: At many destinations, camping is restricted to designated campsites only (see "Destinations" chart below). Additional designated campsites are expected to be created with the expansion of the permit system in 1998, and the chart may not reflect the total number of designated campsites available. Hikers should not camp in stock camps unless the site is double-signed with a hiker camp symbol. Where designated sites are unavailable, camp in well-impacted existing campsites, at a distance from trails and lakeshores to avoid trampling fragile alpine plants. Camping is prohibited within 200 feet of Cradle Lake, Lake Edna, Cup Lake, Larch Lake, and Escondido Tarns.

Party Size: Twelve (combined people and stock). Party size is restricted to 8 persons in the Enchantment Permit Zone. Cross-country travelers are urged to keep party size to 6 people, to avoid damage to fragile natural resources.

▶ **Special Issues:** Wilderness managers are in the midst of developing a phased-in approach to protect the wilderness. The first phase began in 1994 and continues (see "Getting Permits"). Large budget cuts are likely to affect management of this heavily used wilderness, making it particularly important for users to practice low-impact camping techniques in fragile areas and to voluntarily comply with regulations.

Restrictions: Campfires: Prohibited above 4,000 feet west of the Cascade crest (Mt. Baker–Snoqualmie National Forest) and above 5,000 feet east of the crest (Wenatchee National Forest). In addition, campfires are prohibited within 1/2 mile of many lakes below these elevations (see "Destinations" chart below).

Stock: Permitted on many trails; however, to protect water quality, camping with pack and saddle animals is either prohibited or restricted to designated campsites at least 1/2 mile from lakes in a number of locations. Stock are prohibited within 200 feet of lakes, except to water animals or pass on a trail. Do not tie stock to trees under 6 inches in diameter or to a larger tree for more than 4 hours. Hobble horses, mules, donkeys, and burros whenever tied for more than 30 minutes, to prevent pawing. When using a high-line, do not tie animals within 8 feet of a tree unless they are hobbled. Processed feed is required.

DESTINATIONS

NORTH BEND RANGER DISTRICT

Area	Fires	Designated Campsites	Dogs	Stock
Commonwealth Basin	No	No	Leashed	Llamas OK
Denny Creek	No	No	Leashed	Llamas OK
Dutch Miller Gap	Yes*	No	Yes	Llamas OK
Gem Lake	No	For Hikers	Leashed	Llamas OK
Granite Mountain	No	No	Leashed	Llamas OK
Gravel Lake	No	For Hikers	Yes***	Restricted
Island Lake	No	For Hikers	Leashed	No
Lower Tuscohatchie Lk.	No	For Hikers	Leashed	Llamas OK
Mason Lake	No	For Hikers	Leashed	Llamas OK
Melakwa Lake	No	For Hikers	Leashed	Llamas OK
Myrtle Lake	Yes	No	Yes	Llamas OK
Olallie Lake	No	For Hikers	Leashed	Llamas OK
Pratt Lake	No	For Hikers	Leashed	Llamas OK
Rainbow Lake	No	For Hikers	Leashed	Llamas OK
Snow Lake	No	For Hikers	Leashed	Llamas OK
Talapus Lake	No	For Hikers	Leashed	Llamas OK
Williams Lake	No	No	Yes	Llamas OK
Sunday Lake	Yes	No	Yes	Llamas OK
Bare Mountain	Yes*	No	Yes	Llamas OK
Lennox Creek	Yes*	No	Yes	Llamas OK
Snoqualmie Lake	Yes	No	Yes	Llamas OK

SKYKOMISH RANGER DISTRICT

Area	Fires	Designated Campsites	Dogs	Stock
Big Heart Lake	No	For Hikers	Leashed	No
Copper Lake	No	For Hikers	Leashed	No
Deception Lake	No	For Hikers	Yes	Yes
Lake Dorothy	No	For Hikers	Leashed	No
Little Heart Lake	No	For Hikers	Leashed	No

SKYKOMISH RANGER DISTRICT (CONT.)

Malachite Lake	No	For Hikers	Leashed	No
Necklace Valley	No	For Hikers	Leashed	No
Surprise Lake	No	For Hikers	Leashed	No
Tonga Ridge	No	No	Leashed	Yes
Trout Lake	No	For Hikers	Leashed	No

CLE ELUM RANGER DISTRICT

Area	Fires	Designated Campsites	Dogs	Stock
Deep Lake	No	No	Yes	Yes
Escondido Lake	Yes	For Stock	Yes	Yes
Escondido Tarns	No	No	Yes	Restricted
Glacier Lake	No	No	Yes	No
Gold Creek	Yes	No	Leashed	No
Hyas Lake	Yes	No	Yes	Yes
Lake Ivanhoe	No	No	Yes	Restricted
Lake Lillian	Yes	No	Yes	No
Lake Vicente	No	No	Yes	No
Michael Lake	No	For Stock	Yes	Yes
Park Lakes Basin	No	For Stock	Yes	Yes
Pete Lake	Yes	For Stock	Yes	Yes
Rachel Lake	No	No	Yes	No
Rampart Ridge	No	No	Yes	No
Rebecca Lake	No	No	Yes	No
Ridge Lake	No	For Hikers	Yes***	Restricted
Shovel Lake	No	No	Yes	No
Spectacle Lake	No	No	Yes	No
Squaw Lake	Yes	For Stock	Yes	Yes
Terrence Lake	No	No	Yes	No
Waptus Lake	Yes	For Stock	Yes	Yes

LEAVENWORTH RANGER DISTRICT

Area	Fires	Designated Campsites	Dogs	Stock
Caroline Lakes	No	For Hikers and Stock	No	Yes
Chain Lakes	No	For Hikers	Yes	Yes
Chiwaukum Lake	No	No	Yes	No
Colchuck Lake	No	For Hikers	No	No
Cradle Lake	No	No	Yes	Restricted
Doelle Lakes	No	For Hikers and Stock	Yes	Yes
Eightmile Lake	No	No	No	Yes
Enchantment Lakes	No	No	No	No
Flora/Brigham Lakes	No	For Stock	Yes	Yes
Frosty Pass	No	For Stock	Yes	Yes
Headlight Basin	No	For Hikers	No	No
Hope/Mig Lakes	No	No	Yes	Yes
Icicle Creek Trail	Yes**	No	Yes	Yes
Icicle Ridge Trail	No	No	Yes	Yes
Ingalls Creek Trail	Yes**	For Stock	Yes	Yes

LEAVENWORTH RANGER DISTRICT (CONT.)

Ingalls Lake	No	For Hikers	No	No
Jack Creek Trail	Yes**	No	Yes	Yes
osephine Lake	No	No	Yes	Restricted
Junction French/Icicle	No	For Hikers	Yes	Yes
Klonaqua Lake	No	No	Yes	No
Lake Alice	No	No	Yes	Restricted
Lake Margaret	No	No	Yes	Llamas OK
Lake Mary	No	For Hikers	Yes	No
Larch Lake	No	No	Yes	No
Nada Lake	No	For Hikers	No	No
Lake Stuart	No	No	No	No****
Leland Lake	No	No	Yes	No
Little Eightmile Lake	No	No	No	Restricted
Meadow Camp	Yes	For Stock	Yes	Yes
Snow Lakes	No	For Hikers	No	No
Square Lake	No	No	Yes	Restricted
Swimming Deer Lake	No	No	Yes	Yes
Timothy Meadows	Yes	For Stock	Yes	Yes
Trout Lake	No	No	Yes	Yes
Upper Lake Florence	No	For Hikers	Yes	Restricted
Wolverine Lake	No	No	Yes	Restricted

LAKE WENATCHEE RANGER DISTRICT

Area	Fires	Designated Campsites	Dogs	Stock
Deadhorse Pass	No	No	Yes	Yes
Frosty Pass	No	For Stock	Yes	Yes
Lake Donald	No	No	Yes	No
Lake Ethel	No	No	Yes	No
Lake Julius	No	No	Yes	No
Lake Susan Jane	No	No	Yes	Yes
Loch Eileen	No	No	Yes	No
Whitepine Creek	Yes**	No	Yes	Yes
Wildhorse Creek	Yes**	No	Yes	Yes

*Fires permitted below 4,000 feet.

**Fires permitted below 5,000 feet.

***Dogs must be leashed along Pacific Crest Trail north to Mt. Baker–Snoqualmie National Forest boundary.

****Open from the Saturday following Labor Day weekend to January 1.

Leashed = Dogs must be leashed on all trails off I-90 and heavily used trails west of Stevens Pass. Leashing is not required on trails open to saddle and pack animals, except on the PCT north to the Mt. Baker–Snoqualmie National Forest boundary (stock users do not need to leash their dogs on the PCT). Unleashed dogs must be under voice control at all times. Dogs are prohibited in the Enchantment Permit Zone.

Restricted = Stock are permitted but no camping with stock within 1/2 mile of lakes. No camping is available to stock along the PCT between Snoqualmie Pass and Park Lake Basin.

Llamas OK = Llamas and goats permitted but no other saddle or pack animals.

The Mt. Rainier Region

17. Clearwater Wilderness

Administered by the U.S. Forest Service

LOCATION: In Pierce County southeast of Enumclaw near northwest corner of Mt. Rainier National Park.

GENERAL DESCRIPTION: The Clearwater Wilderness includes 14,300 acres of old-growth hemlock-cedar-fir forests which cover most of the wilderness, and small lakes in the Clearwater River and Prairie Creek drainages. There are gorgeous views of Mt. Rainier, but clearcuts on surrounding private and national forest lands do mar some views. There are also spectacular beargrass displays in mid-July on Bearhead Mountain and around Summit Lake.

GETTING THERE: From the west, Interstate 405 south to State Highway 167, then State Highway 410 east through Enumclaw, and Forest Road 74 to trailheads. From the east, pick up Highway 410 at Interstate 82 and drive west to FR 74. **Note:** FR 74 is closed by snow between December 15 and May 1. Users will need to hike into the wilderness during this period. Access also from Carbon River Road 1/4 mile west of the Carbon River entry station to Mt. Rainier National Park. Drive Cayada Creek Road 8 miles to Summit Lake Trailhead. This road presently closed due to flood damage.

NEW IN '98: Trail-Park Pass required for parking at trailheads (see "User Fee" summary on p. 7).

REGULATIONS AT A GLANCE	
User fee	Yes*
Overnight backcountry use permit required	No**
Day use permit required	No**
Party size limit (people and stock)	12

*Trail-Park Pass required for parking at trailheads (see "User Fee" summary on p. 7).
**Voluntary registration encouraged.

ROADSIDE CAMPGROUNDS: There are no campgrounds adjoining the Clearwater Wilderness. The nearest campground is Evans Creek ORV area (27 tent sites, 7 tent/RV sites, can also accommodate groups of up to 24 people). Call ranger district for directions. The Ipsut Creek Campground, 5 miles in from the Carbon River entrance to Mt. Rainier National Park, is also a possibility (29 sites, 2 group camps), but will be walk-in only in 1998 (5 miles) and it is uncertain when road repairs will again allow vehicle access. Call Mt. Rainier National Park for more information on this campground.

NEAREST SERVICES: Greenwater and Enumclaw have gas, food, and lodging.

RANGER DISTRICT

❖ Mt. Baker–Snoqualmie National Forest, **White River Ranger District** (address/phone on p. 93)

Information, trip planning, exhibits, books, maps available.

EMERGENCY CONTACTS: 911; Pierce County Sheriff, (206) 593-4721.

REGULATIONS IN DETAIL

Permit Requirements: None. Please register at the trailhead.

User Fee: Trail-Park Pass required for parking at trailheads (see "User Fee" summary on p. 7).

Backcountry Camping: Permitted throughout the wilderness. Keep 100 feet from lakes and streams. There is a campfire ban within 1/4 mile of the Summit Lake basin. Other restrictions may apply; check with ranger district for details.

Party Size: Twelve (combined people and stock).

▶ Special Issues: The Clearwater Wilderness is habitat for the marbled murrulet, an endangered species. Summit Lake receives very heavy use. The Carbon River Bridge to Cayada Creek Road which provides access to Summit Lake and Bearhead Mountain may be impassable through 1998. Be sure to check in with the ranger station before heading up.

Restrictions: Campfires are permitted except in Summit Lake basin. There is a campfire ban within 1/4 mile of the basin. Where campfires are allowed, use an existing fire ring and dead and downed wood only. Dogs and stock are permitted, but trails are mostly unsuitable for stock. Stock are only permitted on the Summit Lake Trail and must be hitched 200 feet from lakes and streams.

18. Glacier View Wilderness

Administered by the U.S. Forest Service

LOCATION: Pierce County, west of southwestern corner of Mt. Rainier National Park.

GENERAL DESCRIPTION: This 3,080-acre wilderness is small but supplies spectacular views of the glaciated slopes of Mt. Rainier to the east. It was added to the Wilderness System in 1984 to protect and preserve the scenic alpine environment and to complement adjacent Mt. Rainier National Park. Popular destinations include Mt. Beljica (elevation 5,476 feet) and Glacier View Point (elevation 5,507 feet), formerly the site of a 1934 fire lookout.

GETTING THERE: From the west, take State Highway 706, then go north on Forest Road 59 to trailheads.

NEW IN '98: To address the problem of increasing resource damage, the Gifford Pinchot National Forest is proposing a limited permit system for overnight backcountry use of wildernesses it manages. Some changes may take effect in the summer of 1998, with the limited permit system possibly beginning in 1999. Call ranger stations for the most up-to-date information.

REGULATIONS AT A GLANCE

User fee	No
Overnight backcountry use permit required	Yes
Day use permit required	Yes
Permit fee	No
Permit reservations available	No
Use quotas	No
Party size limit (combined people and stock)	12

ROADSIDE CAMPGROUNDS: Sunshine Point, inside Mt. Rainier National Park, near Nisqually entrance (18 tent/RV sites, open year-round, $).

NEAREST SERVICES: Ashford and Elbe have gas, food, and lodging.

RANGER DISTRICT

❖ Gifford Pinchot National Forest, **Packwood Ranger District** (address/phone on p. 92)

Information, trip planning, permits, books, maps, and guides available.

EMERGENCY CONTACTS: 911; Pierce County Sheriff, (206) 593-4721.

REGULATIONS IN DETAIL

Permit Requirements: Required for day and overnight use, one permit per group.
Getting Permits: Permits are available at Packwood Ranger Station or at trailheads.
Backcountry Camping: Permitted. Camp at least 100 feet from lakes.
Party Size: Twelve (combined people and stock).
Restrictions: Campfires are permitted. Use an existing fire ring and dead and downed wood only. Stock are permitted on trails but must be kept at least 200 feet from lakes. Do not tie stock directly to trees. Use a highline, hobble, or moveable picket. Processed feed only. Leashed dogs are allowed on all trails. Caching is allowed for up to 48 hours.

19. Goat Rocks Wilderness

Administered by the U.S. Forest Service

LOCATION: Lewis and Yakima Counties along the crest of the Cascades south of US Highway 12.

GENERAL DESCRIPTION: The 105,633-acre wilderness surrounds Goat Rocks, the craggy remnants of a large, extinct volcano, which was glaciated into several dramatic peaks averaging 8,000 feet high. It was set aside as a primitive area in 1931 and expanded twice before it became a designated wilderness area under the Wilderness Act of 1964. Additional acres were added in 1984.

GETTING THERE: The Pacific Crest Trail can be picked up off Highway 12 at White Pass; numerous forest roads access other trailheads. **Note:** The Yakama Indian Reservation, bordering the Goat Rocks Wilderness on the southeast side, is closed to the public, except for the Pacific Crest Trail route.

NEW IN '98: Trail-Park Pass required for parking at most trailheads (see "User Fee" summary on p. 7). To address the problem of increasing resource damage, the Gifford Pinchot National Forest is proposing a limited permit system for overnight backcountry use of wildernesses it manages. Some changes may take effect in the summer of 1998, with the limited permit system possibly beginning in 1999. Call ranger stations for the most up-to-date information.

REGULATIONS AT A GLANCE

User fee . . . . .Yes*
Overnight backcountry use permit required . . . . .Yes**
Day use permit required . . . . .Yes**
Permit fee . . . . .No
Permit reservations available . . . . .No

Use quotas . . . . .No
Party size limits (combined people and stock) 12
*Trail-Park Pass required to park at most trailheads (see "User Fee" summary on p. 7).
**Trailhead registration.

ROADSIDE CAMPGROUNDS: Walupt Lake Horse Camp (6 sites, $), Walupt Lake (44 sites, $), Scatter Creek (4 sites, $7), White Pass (6 sites, $7).

NEAREST SERVICES: Packwood has gas, food, and lodging; White Pass has gas and food available at Kracker Barrel Store.

RANGER DISTRICTS

❖ Wenatchee National Forest, **Naches Ranger District** (address/phone on p. 95)

❖ Gifford Pinchot National Forest, **Packwood Ranger District** (address/phone on p. 92)

Information, trip planning, books, maps, permits available at both offices.

EMERGENCY CONTACTS: 911; Yakima County Sheriff, (800) 572-0490; Lewis County Sheriff, (360) 748-9286.

REGULATIONS IN DETAIL ▰▰▰▰▰▰▰▰▰▰▰▰▰▰

Permit Requirements: Required for overnight and day use.
Getting Permits: Available from ranger stations and at trailheads.
User Fee: Trail-Park Pass required to park at most trailheads (see "User Fee" summary on p. 7).
Backcountry Camping: Permitted everywhere except at Shoe Lake and Snowgrass Flat. Do not camp within 100 feet of the Pacific Crest Trail or within 100 feet of lake shores.
Party Size: Twelve (combined people and stock).
Restrictions: Shoe Lake Basin and Snowgrass Flat are closed to camping and campfire. Campfires are permitted everywhere except at Shoe Lake, Snowgrass Flat, and Goat Lake. Where permitted, use an existing fire ring and dead and downed wood only. Camp 100 feet from lake shores. Stock are permitted on trails but must be kept at least 200 feet from lakes. Do not tie stock directly to trees. Use a highline, hobble, or moveable picket. Processed feed only. Dogs, under control, are allowed on all trails. Caching is allowed for up to 48 hours.

20. Norse Peak Wilderness
Administered by the U.S. Forest Service

LOCATION: North and east of Mt. Rainier in Pierce and Yakima Counties.

GENERAL DESCRIPTION: Located northeast of Mt. Rainier National Park, north of Chinook Pass State Route 410, along the Pacific Crest Trail through the Cascades, this 50,923-acre wilderness combines an eroded volcanic landscape, forested slopes, a few lakes and tarns, and broad, open grassy basins. The wilderness lies just south of the Naches Pass Trail, cut by pioneers in 1853. The high basins were also used for grazing sheep until the 1940s. Elk now are common through much of the wilderness. Mountain goats inhabit the crags of Castle Mountain and Fifes Peak.

GETTING THERE: In spring, summer, or fall, take SR 410. Trailheads are accessed from SR 410 (lies south of trailheads) and via forest roads on north, east, and west sides. **Note:** Access may be restricted in winter due to closing of Chinook and Cayuse Passes (usually mid-November to Memorial Day weekend), but SR 410 trailheads east of Morse Creek are accessible to vehicles. Winter access is via Morse Creek Road and Crystal Mountain Ski Area.

NEW IN '98: Trail-Park Pass required to park at trailheads (see "User Fee" summary on p. 7).

REGULATIONS AT A GLANCE

User fee . . . . .Yes*
Overnight backcountry use permit required . . . . .No**
Day use permit required . . . . .No
Party size limit (people and stock) 12
*Trail-Park Pass required to park at trailheads (see "User Fee" summary on p. 7).
**Voluntary registration encouraged.

ROADSIDE CAMPGROUNDS: Corral Pass (20 tent/RV sites; off FR 7174); *off SR 410:* Hells Crossing (18 sites, $9), Lodgepole (33 sites, $9), Pleasant Valley (16 sites, $9).

NEAREST SERVICES: Naches, Greenwater, Cliffdell, and Enumclaw have gas, food, and lodging.

RANGER DISTRICTS

❖ Mt. Baker–Snoqualmie National Forest, **White River Ranger District** (address/phone on p. 93)

❖ Wenatchee National Forest, **Naches Ranger District** (address/phone on p. 95)

Information, trip planning, exhibits, books, and maps available at both offices.

EMERGENCY CONTACTS: 911; Pierce County Sheriff, (206) 593-4721; Yakima County Sheriff, (800) 572-0490.

REGULATIONS IN DETAIL

Permit Requirements: None required. Voluntary permits are available at trailheads on east side.

User Fee: Trail-Park Pass required to park at primary trailheads (see "User Fee" summary on p. 7).

Backcountry Camping: Permitted throughout the wilderness, except within 100 feet of the Pacific Crest Trail. Select campsites at least 100 feet from lake shores.

Party Size: Twelve (combined people and stock).

♦ Special Issues: Non-hunters may want to wear bright clothing in this area during the regular deer and elk season, which runs from mid-October to mid-November. The Greenwater Road (70) was washed out by flooding in November 1995 at milepost 6.7. Reconstruction of this stretch is expected to be completed by fall 1998. Until then, the Greenwater trailhead and the Naches Pass area are not accessible. A bypass road owned and maintained by Plum Creek Co. is not recommended for public use.

Restrictions: Campfires are permitted. Use an existing fire ring and dead and downed wood only. Camp 100 feet from lake shores (in and out of the wilderness). Dogs and stock are permitted. Pack and saddle stock must be kept at least 200 feet from lakes. Do not tie stock directly to trees. Use a highline, hobble, or moveable picket.

21. Tatoosh Wilderness

Administered by the U.S. Forest Service

LOCATION: South of Mt. Rainier National Park in Lewis County.

GENERAL DESCRIPTION: This 15,800-acre wilderness is steep and rugged with sub-alpine and alpine areas along the ridge line. Tatoosh Ridge (elevation 6,310 feet), the former site of a 1932 fire lookout, offers 360-degree views, including Mt. Rainier.

GETTING THERE: From Packwood take Forest Road 52, then FR 5270 and 5290 to trailheads.

NEW IN '98: To address the problem of increasing resource damage, the Gifford Pinchot National Forest is proposing a limited permit system for overnight backcountry use of wildernesses it manages. Some changes may take effect in the summer of 1998, with the limited permit system possibly beginning in 1999. Call ranger stations for the most up-to-date information.

REGULATIONS AT A GLANCE

User fee	No
Overnight backcountry use permit required	Yes
Day use permit required	Yes
Permit fee	No
Permit reservations available	No
Use quotas	No
Party size limit (combined people and stock)	12

ROADSIDE CAMPGROUNDS: Nearest campground is La Wis Wis, 7 miles northeast of Packwood, then 1/2 mile on Forest Road 1272 (100 tent/RV sites, $).

NEAREST SERVICES: Packwood has gas, food, and lodging.

RANGER DISTRICT

❖ Gifford Pinchot National Forest, **Packwood Ranger District** (address/phone on p. 92)

Information, trip planning, books, maps, and permits available.

EMERGENCY CONTACTS: 911; Lewis County Sheriff, (360) 748-8887.

REGULATIONS IN DETAIL

Permit Requirements: Required for day and overnight use, free, one permit per group (see "NEW IN '98").

Getting Permits: Permits are available from Packwood Ranger Station and at trailheads.

Backcountry Camping: Permitted throughout the wilderness, except in Tatoosh Lakes Basin. Select campsites at least 100 feet from lakes.

Party Size: Twelve (combined people and stock).

Restrictions: Campfires are permitted throughout the wilderness, except in Tatoosh Lakes Basin. Use an existing fire ring and dead and downed wood only. Stock are permitted on all trails, except Tatoosh Lakes Trail, due to steep grades and poor condition. Stock are also not recommended on the West Side Trail. Keep pack and saddle stock at least 200 feet from lakes. Do not tie stock directly to trees. Use a highline, hobble, or moveable picket. Processed feed only. Dogs are permitted on trails. Caching is allowed for up to 48 hours.

22. William O. Douglas Wilderness

Administered by the U.S. Forest Service

LOCATION: Lewis and Yakima Counties, mainly on the east side of the Cascade crest, between the American and Tieton Rivers (between Chinook Pass State Route 410 and White Pass U.S. Highway 12).

GENERAL DESCRIPTION: The William O. Douglas Wilderness is named for the conservation-minded Supreme Court justice who had a cabin at Goose Prairie. Douglas hiked extensively throughout the area for years and wrote about it in his book *Of Men and Mountains*.

Consisting of two broad, high ridge complexes astride the Cascades, on either side of the Bumping River drainage, this 167,195-acre wilderness encompasses rivers, streams, lakes, craggy peaks, wooded plateaus, meadows, both dry-side and wet-side plants, some mountain goats, and large herds of elk and mule deer that winter along the eastern slopes. Eastern portions (Meeks Table) host eastside pine stands. The Pacific Crest Trail runs north–south along its western backbone.

GETTING THERE: State Route 410, US Highway 12, and numerous forest roads to trailheads and campgrounds.

NEW IN '98: Trail-Park Pass required to park at trailheads in Wenatchee NF (but not at the four trailheads entering from Gifford Pinchot NF—Carlton Creek, Cartright, Sand Lake, and the Soda Springs area). (See "User Fee" summary on p. 7.)

REGULATIONS AT A GLANCE

User fee . . . . .Yes*
Overnight backcountry use permit required . . . . .Yes**
Day use permit required . . . . .Yes**
Permit fee . . . . .No
Use quotas . . . . .No
Party size limit (combined people and stock) 12

*Trail-Park Pass required to park at trailheads in Wenatchee NF (see "NEW IN '98" above).
**Trailhead registration.

ROADSIDE CAMPGROUNDS: *Off Bumping Road, FS 1800:* Bumping Crossing (12 sites), Bumping Lake (45 sites, $9/11), Cougar Flat (12 sites, $9), Cedar Springs (15 sites, $9), Soda Springs (8 sites, $9); *off State Route 410:* Halfway Flat (12 sites, $7), Hells Crossing (17 sites, $9), Little Naches (21 sites, $9), Lodgepole (33 sites, $9), Pleasant Valley (16 sites, $9), Sawmill Flat (24 sites, $9); *off U.S. Highway 12:* Clear Lake North (34 sites, $9), Clear Lake South (23 sites, $9), Dog Lake (11 sites, $5, closed to horses), Hause Creek (42 sites, $9), White Pass (16 sites, $7), Summit Creek (7 sites).

NEAREST SERVICES: Packwood has gas, food, and lodging.

RANGER DISTRICTS

❖ Gifford Pinchot National Forest, **Packwood Ranger District** (address/phone on p. 92)

❖ Wenatchee National Forest, **Naches Ranger District** (address/phone on p. 95)

Information, books, maps, and permits are available at both offices.

EMERGENCY CONTACTS: 911; Yakima County Sheriff, (800) 572-0490; Lewis County Sheriff, (360) 748-8887.

REGULATIONS IN DETAIL

Permit Requirements: Required for all day and overnight use, one permit per group.
Getting Permits: Available free from Packwood Ranger Station and Naches Ranger Station and at trailheads.
User Fee: Trail-Park Pass required to park at trailheads in Wenatchee NF (but not at the four trailheads entering from Gifford Pinchot NF—Carlton Creek, Cartright, Sand Lake, and the Soda Springs area). (See "User Fee" summary on p.7.)
Backcountry Camping: Permitted throughout the wilderness, except within 100 feet of the Pacific Crest National Scenic Trail. Select campsites at least 100 feet from lakes.
Party Size: Twelve (combined people and stock).
Restrictions: Campfires are permitted, except at Dewey Lakes. Use an existing fire ring and dead and downed wood only. Camp 100 feet from lake shores. Stock are permitted on trails, except at Goat Peak and Big Twin Sister, but are not recommended on Carlton Creek Trail. Stock must be kept at least 200 feet from lakes. Do not tie stock directly to trees. Use a highline, hobble, or moveable picket. Processed feed only. Dogs, under control, are permitted on trails. Caching is allowed for up to 48 hours.

23. Mt. Rainier National Park

Administered by the National Park Service

LOCATION: Southeast of Tacoma in Pierce and Lewis Counties, surrounding Mt. Rainier.

GENERAL DESCRIPTION: Washington's highest peak and its most popular, 14,411-foot Mt. Rainier looms to the southeast over the city of Seattle. The perennially glacier-clad mountain, one of Washington's espisodically active Cascade volcanoes, lures thousands of climbers each year over scores of glaciers, rivers, and steep-walled canyons as they attempt to reach the summit. There are more than 240 miles of maintained trails criss-crossing densely forested slopes and wildflower-strewn subalpine meadows, which are home to black bear, hoary marmot, mountain goats, and other wildlife. Almost 97% of 236,612-acre Mt. Rainier National Park is designated wilderness, and much of the park is bordered by adjoining wilderness areas administered by the U.S. Forest Service.

GETTING THERE: The park can be entered by road from the northwest (Mowich/Carbon River), northeast and east (Sunrise), southeast (Ohanapecosh/Stevens Canyon), and southwest (Nisqually). Gray Line Tours of Seattle also runs buses to the park between mid-spring and mid-fall; for the schedule, call (800) 426-7532. Rainier Overland, (360) 569-0851, and Rainier Shuttle, Inc., (360) 569-2331, both operate a shuttle between SeaTac Airport and Mt. Rainier. Call for schedules. There is no public transportation within the park. All park roads are closed in winter (roughly October 1–June 30, depending on snowfall), except between the Nisqually entrance and Paradise and from the park boundary to Ohanapecosh Ranger Station. State Route 410 and SR-123 frequently open late April/early May, Stevens Canyon by Memorial Day, and Sunrise in very late June. In winter the gate to Paradise Road at Longmire is usually open by 8:00 A.M. if there is no snow. If the road must be plowed, it may not be passable until the afternoon. Cayuse Pass and Chinook Pass on the east side of the mountain generally close in late

November and reopen sometime in early June, depending on snowmelt. **Note:** The Westside Road is closed to vehicles from milepost 3.2 until further notice due to repeated washouts. Hikers, bicyclists, and leashed dogs may be allowed beyond that point, depending on conditions along Tahoma Creek. Bicycles and leashed dogs are allowed only on the road surface, not on trails or off the road surface. Carbon River Road is also closed to vehicles due to storm damage. Hiking and bicycling are allowed beyond the closure, with the same bicycle rules as for the Westside Road. The gravel road to Mowich Lake in the northwest corner of the park normally opens the first week in July (opening may be delayed by late snow melt) and is closed the second week of October or with the first significant snowfall (whichever comes soonest!).

SPECIALIZED MAPS: Trails Illustrated™ maps: Mt. Rainier National Park.

REGULATIONS AT A GLANCE

User fee . . . . .No
Overnight permit required for backpacking . . . . .Yes
Day use wilderness permit required . . . . .No
Climbing permits and cards . . . . .Yes
Wilderness camping permit fee . . . . .No*
Climbing permit fee . . . . .Yes
Permit reservations available . . . . .No*
Use quotas . . . . .By area
Party size limit on trails (when using group campsites) .12
Party size limit on trails (when using individual sites) . . . . 5, or 1 family
Cross-country party size limit . . . . .Varies**
*Wilderness camping fees and permit reservations may go into effect the summer of 1998. Check with Information Centers.
**5 in lower elevation areas/5 on bare ground or 12 on snow in alpine areas

ROADSIDE CAMPGROUNDS

South: Sunshine Point (18 individual sites, year-round, $) near the Nisqually entrance; Cougar Rock (200 individual sites, 5 group sites, $), 2.5 miles from Longmire on Paradise Road.

Southeast: Ohanapecosh (205 individual sites, $) in the southeast corner of the park.

Northwest: Ipsut Creek (29 individual sites, 2 group sites, $), at end of Carbon River Road. (Ipsut Creek Campground will be walk-in only in 1998 [5 miles]. It is uncertain when road repairs will again allow vehicle access.) Mowich Lake, at the end of the Mowich Lake Road, has approximately 30 undesignated walk-in sites in an old road turn-around.

East: White River (117 individual sites, $) off White River Road.

Group campsites may be reserved by calling the ranger secretary at (360) 569-2211, ext. 3301.

NEAREST SERVICES: Within the park, food and lodging are available at Paradise (summer only) and at the National Park Inn at Longmire (year-round). Food is available at Sunrise, summer only. Outside the park, gas, food, and lodging are available in Ashford, Packwood, Yakima, Enumclaw, Wilkeson, and Fairfax. No gasoline is available in the park.

RANGER STATIONS
Mt. Rainier National Park Headquarters
Tahoma Woods, Star Route
Ashford, WA 98304
(360) 569-2211

Ranger Stations (South Side)
Nisqually Ranger Station . . . .(360) 569-2211, ext. 2390
Longmire Ranger Station . . . .(360) 569-2211, ext. 3305
Paradise Ranger Station . . . .(360) 569-2211, ext. 2314

Ranger Stations (North and East Sides—summer only)
Wilkeson Ranger Station . . . .(360) 829-5127
White River Ranger Station . . . .(360) 569-2211, ext. 2356, or (360) 663-2273
Sunrise Ranger Station . . . .(360) 569-2211, ext. 2357, or (360) 663-2425
Ohanapecosh Ranger Station . . . .(360) 569-2211, ext. 2352
Note: Wilderness ranger stations are unstaffed.

INFORMATION CENTERS
(South Side)
Henry M. Jackson Memorial Visitor Center, Paradise
(360) 569-2211, ext. 2328

Books, maps, interpretive programs, exhibits, summer naturalist walks and winter snow-
shoe hikes, ranger information. Wilderness and climbing permits. Open daily early
May through mid-October. Open Sat./Sun./Holidays only mid-October through
April.

Ohanapecosh Visitor Center (summer only)
(360) 569-2211, ext. 2352, or (360) 494-2229

Books, maps, interpretive programs, exhibits, summer naturalist walks, information, and
wilderness permits. Open early June through early October.

Longmire Wilderness Center
(360) 569-2211, ext. 3317

Relief map of Mt. Rainier, wilderness permits, climbing permits, trip planning, multimedia
CD-ROM Wilderness Education touch-screen program. Open mid-June through
September 30. Obtain permits from Longmire Museum beginning October 1.

INFORMATION CENTERS
(East Side)
Sunrise Visitor Center (summer only)
(360) 569-2211, ext. 2357, or (360) 663-2425

Information, exhibits, interpretive programs.

White River Hiker Information Center/Ranger Station (summer only)
(360) 569-2211, ext. 2356, or (360) 663-2273

Wilderness permits, climbing permits, trip planning. After September 29, obtain permits
from U.S. Forest Service White River Ranger Station in Enumclaw.

EMERGENCY CONTACTS: 911; National Park Service, (360) 569-2211.

REGULATIONS IN DETAIL

Use Quotas: Camp Schurman and Camp Muir are heavily used by climbers. Quotas are based on number of people, not number of parties entering those areas: 35 for Camp Schurman and 110 for Camp Muir. Other popular areas are Indian Bar (3 individual sites, 1 group site), Summerland (5 individual sites, 1 group site), and Mystic (7 individual sites, 2 group sites).

Permit Requirements: Permits are required for all overnight wilderness use.

Getting Permits: Permits are obtainable from ranger stations, visitor centers, and wilderness information centers throughout the park. At present reservations for designated wilderness camps are not available in advance, but a reservation system may be in effect by summer of 1998 (check with information centers for latest information). Climbing cards are required for persons climbing above 10,000 feet or on glaciers. One-time cost is $15 per permit, or $25 for an annual climbing card. Register with a park ranger before and after the trip.

Wilderness Camping: Designated wilderness camps are assigned at the time the permit is issued. Camps are more likely to fill Friday/Saturday, but can also fill any night, especially during August. Backpackers may need to accept second- or third-choice campsites on some nights, so have alternate campsites in mind when getting permits. Try to arrange your trip to begin between Sunday and Thursday to have the best chance of getting a permit for your desired camp(s). Campers in Camp Schurman are required to use a "blue bag" for all human waste and dispose of it in a barrel provided for that purpose .

Trailside Camping: Permitted in designated camps only, on maintained trails. Parties of 1–5 people with up to two tents may camp in an individual site; parties of 6–12 must use a designated group campsite. Large parties cannot be split into small groups at camps. Boil, filter, or otherwise treat all water before use.

Cross-Country Camping: Cross-country backpackers may camp in cross-country or alpine zones, at least 1/4 mile from the trail and 100 feet from any water source, using minimum-impact camping techniques. The number of parties allowed in fragile subalpine zones (5,000–7,000 feet) is restricted. Between June 1 and September 30, all cross-country campers must stay 1/4 mile from roads and trails and at least 100 feet from lakes, streams, and wetlands. Parties are restricted to 5 people or 1 immediate family (if camping on snow in alpine areas above 7,000 feet, the limit is 12). There is no restriction on the number of parties that may use lower forest zones, but campers must stay 1/4 mile from the trail and 100 feet from water. Boil, filter, or treat all water before use.

Alpine Camping: Climbers and alpine hikers using areas above treeline (generally 6,000 feet) or on exposed rock, glaciers, and snowfields must camp on permanent snow or ice or on bare ground previously used as a campsite. Group size is limited to 12 for camping on snow and ice and 5 for bare ground areas. Camping is prohibited within the boundaries of the Muir snowfield between Pebble Creek and Anvil Rock, the Paradise area and Burroughs Mountain. Carry an altimeter to ensure accurate elevation, as well as a map and compass. Climbing cards (see "Getting Permits" above) are required for camping above Camp Muir and Camp Schurman.

Winter Camping: Between October 1 and May 31, campsites must be 200 feet from plowed roads and 100 feet from lakes and streams and be on at least 2 feet of snow. Group size may be as many as 12. Camping at Paradise is allowed when there is at least 5 feet of snow on the ground, subject to the above restrictions. Groups over 12 in number are permitted but must camp 300–600 feet from restrooms and are required to use them.

Party Size: Twelve people maximum at wilderness group sites. Larger parties will not be able to find designated group campsites in the wilderness. Large parties may not split into small groups at camps; this is to prevent social trails forming between camps. Individual wilderness sites accommodate up to 5 people with two tents. Cross-country backpackers must restrict party size to 5 people or 1 immediate family. Parties with stock may not exceed 12 pairs of eyes on the PCT; on other trails, a maximum of 5 people/5 stock is permitted in individual sites and 12 people/5 stock at group sites.

▶ **Special Issues:** Human waste disposal is a problem at Camp Schurman in the high country. Campers are required to pick up a "blue bag" for human waste at time of permitting. Bags may be disposed of in barrels located at Ingraham Flats, Camp Shurman, and Camp Muir.

Restrictions: Campfires: Prohibited, except in fireplaces in roadside camping areas.

Dogs: Prohibited on all trails; permitted on leash in roadside campgrounds. Owners will receive a citation if animals are left unattended or allowed to disturb others.

Caching: Prohibited. Food storage is permitted, however. Store food in secure containers and hang at least 12 feet high and 10 feet away from tree trunks to deter animals. To keep down backpack weight, hikers on the Wonderland Trail may send ahead or drop off provisions at ranger stations along the route for pick-up. Pack food in rodent-proof containers and label with name, cache station, and pick-up date. Call the park for cache locations.

Stock: Trails suitable for stock are North Puyallup, Naches Peak, Eastside, Laughing Water Creek, and Rampart Bridge. Stock are allowed on the following portions of the Wonderland Trail: Longmire to Rampart Bridge, North Puyallup River to Mowich Lake, Mowich Lake to Carbon River, Box Canyon to Reflection Lakes, and Reflection Lakes to Longmire. Stock are permitted only in Deer Creek, Three Lakes, Mowich River, and North Puyallup trailside camps. Stock are not permitted within 100 yards of trail shelters or wilderness campsites. Do not use stock on park trails until early August as trails are muddy or may be snow-covered before then. To prevent the spread of exotic plants, stock should be fed compact feed for at least 2 days prior to entry into park. Processed feed is required within the park. Stock may be loaded or unloaded only at points where designated stock trails cross roadways and adequate parking exists.

INTERNET: Mt. Rainier National Park Home Page: http://www.nps.gov/nira/

MOUNT ST. HELENS/MT. ADAMS REGION

24. Indian Heaven Wilderness

Administered by the U.S. Forest Service

LOCATION: Southwest of Mt. Adams in Skamania County.

GENERAL DESCRIPTION: Set on a forested plateau between the White Salmon and Wind Rivers in southern Washington, 20,690-acre Indian Heaven Wilderness is a varied landscape of gentle terrain, lakes, marshes, meadows, and volcanic cones and craters. Tribal people have hunted, fished, and picked huckleberries here for thousands of years, and it was for them that the wilderness was named. Indian Racetrack, where native people gathered to socialize and hold pony races, is an area of unusual archeological interest in the southwestern portion of the wilderness.

GETTING THERE: From the southwest and southeast, take State Highway 14 to White Salmon (then north on State Highway 141 to Trout Lake—visitors coming through Trout Lake can stop and pick up information at the Trout Lake Ranger Station) or to Carson (then Forest Road 65 to westside trailheads or take FR 66 and pick up FR 6035 to eastside trailheads and campgrounds). From the north, use FR 24 and 30. From the east, take FR 24 from Trout Lake and pick up FR 6035. (Visitors coming from this direction can stop and pick up information at the Trout Lake Ranger Station.) The PCT also runs north–south through the Wilderness, crossing FR 24 and 60.

NEW IN '98: Trail-Park Pass required for parking at the Placid Lake and Thomas Lake trailheads (see "User Fee" summary on p. 7). To address the problem of increasing resource damage, the Gifford Pinchot National Forest is proposing a limited permit system for overnight backcountry use of wildernesses it manages. Some changes may take effect in the summer of 1998, with the limited permit system possibly beginning in 1999. Call ranger stations for the most up-to-date information.

REGULATIONS AT A GLANCE

User fee	Yes*
Wilderness permits required	Yes
Climbing permits and cards	No
Permit fee	No
Permit reservations available	No
Use quotas	See below
Party size limit (combined people and stock)	12

*Trail-Park Pass required for parking at the Placid Lake and Thomas Lake trailheads (see "User Fee" summary on p. 7).

ROADSIDE CAMPGROUNDS: Goose Lake (25 tent sites, 1 RV site, $), Forlorn Lakes (8 sites), Smoky Creek (3 RV-only sites), Little Goose Horse Camp (3 sites), Little Goose (28 sites), Cultus Creek (51 sites, $), and Falls Creek Horse Camp (6 sites). Peterson Prairie Group Camp (off FR 24, $) and Atkisson Group Camp (off Highway 141, $), with space for 1 group each, are the closest group camps. Make reservations by calling (800) 280-CAMP.

NEAREST SERVICES: Trout Lake and Carson have gas, food, and lodging.

RANGER DISTRICT

❖ Gifford Pinchot National Forest, **Mt. Adams Ranger District,** Trout Lake (address/phone on p. 92)

Information, books, trail guides, permits, and maps available.

EMERGENCY CONTACTS: 911.

REGULATIONS IN DETAIL ▬▬▬▬▬▬▬▬▬▬▬▬▬▬▬▬▬

Use Quotas: The number of overnight use permits may be limited beginning in 1998.

Permit Requirements: Wilderness permits are required for both day and overnight use.

Getting Permits: Permits are available free from trailheads and from Mt. Adams Ranger Station in Trout Lake.

User Fee: Trail-Park Pass required for parking at the Placid Lake and Thomas Lake trailheads (see "User Fee" summary on p. 7).

Backcountry Camping:

Permitted throughout the wilderness. Campers are urged to camp 100 feet from lakes and streams, or preferably at existing campsites, which may be closer to shorelines.

Party Size: Twelve (combined people and stock).

Stock: Permitted on all trails. Keep animals 200 feet from lakes and streams. Do not tie directly to trees. Use a highline, hobble, or moveable picket. Certified weed-free processed feed only.

▶ **Special Issues:** Trails get very muddy; it is suggested that stock be used only during dry conditions to avoid damaging trails and degrading fragile meadows.

Restrictions: Campfires are permitted throughout the wilderness. Use an existing fire ring and dead and downed wood only. Dogs are allowed on trails. Caching is prohibited.

25. Mt. Adams Wilderness

Administered by the U.S. Forest Service

LOCATION: South-central Washington in Yakima and Skamania Counties.

GENERAL DESCRIPTION: Named for 12,276-foot Mt. Adams, the second tallest of Washington's volcanoes, this 47,280-acre wilderness in the southern portion of the state is less well known but no less dramatic. Thick evergreen forests lap the lower elevations, giving way to heavily glaciated valleys on the west and east sides of the Cascades. Numerous creek drainages radiate from the summit, providing good hiking and climbing trails that link with the main north–south Pacific Crest Trail. An accessible lava bed lies on the more gently sloped south side, offering a rare look at post-eruption geological and botanical features. Entry into the eastern portion of the Mt. Adams Wilderness is via a few short trails located within Tract D of the Yakama Indian Reservation. Users must obtain a separate permit for this section from the Yakama Nation before entering. Climbing Mt. Adams on the east side is not recommended due to hazardous conditions.

GETTING THERE: From the southwest, take State Highway 14 east along the Columbia River to White Salmon, then go north on State Highway 141 to Trout Lake. Forest Road 23 then continues north to the west side of the Wilderness and trailheads, and FR 80 and 82 and several minor forest roads access trails on the south side. To reach the east side (Tract D of the Yakama Indian Reservation), turn east from Highway 141 at Trout Lake and continue on Trout Lake Highway to Glenwood. Mt. Adams Highway then stretches north. Take FR 82 and 8200 series to the Mirror Lake area. **Note:** This area is closed from September 30 until July 1, during which time gates on roads are closed and locked. When the area is open, permits must be purchased for entry (see "Permit Requirements" and "Getting Permits" below). To reach the east side from the north, go east on Highway 12 to Yakima, then drop south on Highway 97, turn west on Highway 142 at Goldendale, and head toward Glenwood. From the north, take I-5 south and turn east on Highway 12 to Randle, then take FR 23 south to the west side of Mt. Adams. The Pacific Crest Trail also enters the wilderness from the north and south.

Roads throughout the area are long, and you should enter with a full tank of gas. Local gas stations are likely to be closed in the evening. RVs are common on roads and can sharply increase travel times. Be advised that roads on the east side are poorly maintained and four-wheel-drive and high-clearance vehicles are recommended. Running water is only sporadically available; bring water and supplies with you.

NEW IN '98: Trail-Park Pass required for parking at most trailheads (see "User Fee" summary on p. 7). To address the problem of increasing resource damage, the Gifford Pinchot National Forest is proposing a limited permit system for overnight backcountry use of wildernesses it manages. Some changes may take effect in the summer of 1998, with the limited permit system possibly beginning in 1999. A proposal is also being considered to put in a quota system for the south climb up Mt. Adams, which may go into effect in 1998. Call ranger stations for the most up-to-date information.

REGULATIONS AT A GLANCE

User fee . . . . .Yes*
Wilderness permit required . . . . .Yes
Climbing permits and cards . . . . .Yes**
Permit fee*** . . . . .No
Use quotas**** . . . . .No
Party size limit (combined people and stock) 12
*Trail-Park Pass required for parking at most trailheads (see "User Fee" summary on p. 7).
**Climbers are encouraged (but not required) to sign in and out at Ranger Station Climbing Register for safety reasons. Currently only Wilderness Permits are required.
***No fee for USFS permits; fees charged for using Tract D lands of Yakama Indian Reservation.
****Use quotas are subject to change in 1998. Call ranger stations before departure.

ROADSIDE CAMPGROUNDS: Horseshoe Lake (10 sites), Killen Creek (8 sites), Takhlakh Lake (54 sites, $), Olallie Lake (5 sites), Council Lake (11 sites), Morrison Creek (12 sites). North Fork Group Camp is located off FR 23 (3 sites: 40, 40, and 25 people maximum in each, $). To reserve, call (800) 280-CAMP.

NEAREST SERVICES: Trout Lake and Randle have gas, food, and lodging. Lodging at Trout Lake is bed and breakfast only.

RANGER DISTRICTS/INFORMATION CENTERS

❖ Gifford Pinchot National Forest, **Mt. Adams Ranger District,** Trout Lake (address/phone on p. 92)

❖ Gifford Pinchot National Forest, **Randle Ranger District** (address/phone on p. 92)

Yakama Nation Forestry Development Program
P.O. Box 151
Toppenish, WA 98948
(509) 865-5121, ext. 657

Information, permits, trail guides, maps, and books are available at ranger stations.
Information on accessing Yakama Indian Reservation lands is available from the
Yakama Nation's Forestry Development Program office.

EMERGENCY CONTACTS: 911; Yakima County Sheriff, (800) 572-0490.

REGULATIONS IN DETAIL

Use Quotas: Overnight camping may be limited in the wilderness on Gifford Pinchot
National Forest lands in 1998, due to impacts related to heavy use. A proposal is being
considered to put in a quota system for the south climb up Mt Adams, which may go into
effect in 1998. Contact the ranger district for most up-to-date information.

Overnight backcountry users, accessing Mt. Adams from the Yakama Reservation
on the east side, should note that camping is allowed in designated campsites only
between July 1 and September 30 (reservation lands are closed the rest of the year).
Permits are issued daily on site, on a first-come, first-served basis, for a set fee. The
number of designated campsites available is as follows: 44 campsites at Bench Lake,
22 campsites at Bird Lake, 6 campsites at Mirror Lake, and 12 campsites at Sunrise
Camp at Mazama.

Permit Requirements: Required for entering Mt. Adams Wilderness and for entering
Tract D of the Yakama Indian Reservation (east side). Tract D is open only between July 1
and September 30, and backcountry day and overnight use permits are required for all visitors. Fees are collected on site by uniformed gatekeepers, who issue a receipt for your
dashboard. Consider cutting costs by carpooling.

Getting Permits: Permits are available free from trailheads and from Mt. Adams and
Randle Ranger Stations. A separate permit from the Yakama Indian Nation is required for
entry into the east side of Mt. Adams on the Yakama Indian Reservation (see "User Fee"
below for details). Overnight permits are issued on a first-come, first-served basis for designated campsites only (accommodating approximately 8 people per campsite). For those
accessing Tract D from the Round-the-Mountain Trail, permits are available from staff in
the Bird Creek Meadows area. For more help on trip planning, contact the Forestry
Development Program office of the Yakama Nation at (509) 865-5121, ext. 657, before
departure.

Those wishing to climb Mt. Adams should register before and after their trip at
either Randle or Mt. Adams Ranger Stations. Wilderness permits are required for the
climb, but climbing permits (and quotas) are not currently in effect. However, a proposal is being considered to put in a quota system for the south climb up Mt. Adams,
which may go into effect in 1998. Call ranger stations for the most current information before departure.

User Fee: Trail-Park Pass required for parking at most trailheads (see "User Fee" summary on p. 7).

A permit from the Yakama Indian Nation is required for entry into the east side of
Mt. Adams on the Yakama Indian Reservation. Day users pay a $5-per-car gate fee for
an 8-hour stay. Overnight users pay a $10-per-car gate fee for a 24-hour stay. A fee
for fishing is also charged: $5 per day or $10 for 7 days. Season permits are available:

$25 per person for hiking and camping, $15 per person for fishing.

Backcountry Camping: Allowed throughout the wilderness. Camp in previously used sites and remain 100 feet from the PCT and shorelines. On the Yakama Reservation, camping is allowed in designated campsites only. Divide Camp, Killen Creek, and High Camp Trails in the northern section of Mt. Adams are heavily used trails. Visitors who can schedule their trips during mid-week will find greater opportunities for solitude.

Party Size: Twelve (combined humans and stock).

▶ **Special Issues:** Water is a particular problem in the area. Be sure to filter or treat all water, especially at heavily used hiking or climbing areas. Human waste is often evident at the "Lunch Counter" (9,000 feet elevation on the South Climb route), where altitude and temperature delay decomposition. Camps above treeline may be affected by high winds that cause "sand storms" of volcanic sand and pumice, which can ruin cameras, carabiners, zippers, and other equipment. Take extra care when camping at these elevations. Please do not build additional rock shelters! Over 260 campsites have been identified on the South Climb. Note, too, that the Muddy Meadows, Killen Creek, and Divide Camp trail systems on the northern side of Mt. Adams are particularly muddy in spring and unsuitable for stock.

Restrictions: Campfires are permitted, except above timberline (approximately 6,000 feet), e.g., above the Round-the-Mountain Trail from the national forest boundary west to the PCT; above the PCT, north to the intersection of the Highline Trail; and above the Highline Trail, north and east to the national forest boundary. Stock are permitted on all trails, although northside trails may be very muddy and impassable in spring. Tethering or grazing of stock is prohibited within 200 feet of lakes. Do not tie animals directly to trees. Use a highline, hobble, or moveable picket. Certified weed-free, processed feed only. Caching is permitted for up to 48 hours.

26. Mount St. Helens National Volcanic Monument

Trail Guide administered by the U.S. Forest Service

LOCATION: 40 miles northeast of Portland, Oregon, in portions of Lewis, Cowlitz, Skamania, and Clark Counties.

GENERAL DESCRIPTION: One of many Cascade Range volcanoes, 8,365-foot Mount St. Helens erupted dramatically on May 18, 1980, devastating a surrounding area of 200-plus square miles. Since 1982, the 110,000-acre Mount St. Helens National Volcanic Monument has protected the blast zone, allowing for natural recovery of the area, scientific research, and visitor education and recreation. The completion of State Highway 504 from Coldwater Lake to Johnston Ridge and the opening of the Johnston Ridge Observatory in May 1997 resulted in expanded day hiking, cross-monument hiking, and backcountry hiking opportunities with the opening of the Hummocks, South Coldwater, and Boundary Trails. The monument is a designated pilot fee demonstration area and user fees are in effect for developed sites, for climbing permits for Mount St. Helens, and for camping permits for Mount Margaret Backcountry.

GETTING THERE: Take State Highway 504 and Forest Roads 25, 81, 83, 90, 99, and minor forest roads to trailheads. The main trailhead for climbers is at Climber's Bivouac on the south side of the mountain off FR 83. After registering and picking up a required climbing permit, take Highway 503 to FR 90, then FR 83 to 830. Dispersed camping, toilets, and emergency phone are available here. The main trailhead for winter climbers is the Marble Mountain Sno-Park, the plowed terminus of FR 83.

NEW IN '98: Beginning in late 1998, a limited number of camping permits will be available for overnight stays in the Mount Margaret Backcountry. Camping will be allowed in designated sites only and party size for this area will also be restricted. For further details, contact Monument Headquarters at (360) 247-3900.

REGULATIONS AT A GLANCE

User fee . . . . .No*
Camping permits required for Mount Margaret Backcountry . . . . .Yes
Day use permit required . . . . .By area
Climbing permits and registration . . . . .Yes
Permit fee . . . . .Yes
Permit reservations available . . . . .Yes
Use quotas . . . . .By area
Party size limit . . . . .By area
*See below regarding visitor center, Mount Margaret Backcountry, and climbing fees.

ROADSIDE CAMPGROUNDS: Lower Falls (43 sites, $) on FR-90, Iron Creek (98 sites, $) on FR-25. **Note:** Iron Creek campsites can be reserved; call (800) 280-CAMP. There are horse camps at Kalama (10 sites) on FR-81 and Lewis River (6 sites) on FR-90. Group campsites are available in nearby Pacific Power and Light and state park campgrounds.

NEAREST SERVICES: Castle Rock, Randle, Morton, Packwood, Cougar, Woodland, and Kelso/Longview have gas, food, and lodging.

RANGER DISTRICTS
Gifford Pinchot National Forest

Mount St. Helens National Volcanic Monument
42218 NE Yale Bridge Road
Amboy, WA 98601
(360) 247-3900 (Information on conditions and road closures)
(360) 247-3903 (24-hour recording)
(360) 247-3902 (TTY)
(360) 247-3961 (Climbing Information Line)

INFORMATION CENTERS
Mount St. Helens Visitor Center
3029 Spirit Lake Highway
Castle Rock, WA 98611
(360) 274-2100

The Mount St. Helens Visitor Center is at milepost 5 along State Route 504, the Coldwater Ridge Visitor Center is at milepost 43, and the Johnston Ridge Observatory is at milepost 52.

The visitor centers offer information on road and trail conditions, closures, and volcanic activity, as well as trip planning, exhibits, books, maps, and interpretive programs.

They are open daily, year-round, except Thanksgiving, Christmas, and New Year's Day.

Summer hours (May 1–September 30): 9:00 A.M.–6:00 P.M. at Mount St. Helens Visitor Center, Coldwater Ridge Visitor Center, and Johnston Ridge Observatory. Winter hours (October 1–March 31): 9:00 A.M.–5:00 P.M.

EMERGENCY CONTACTS: 911; Cowlitz County Sheriff, (360) 577-3092; Lewis County Sheriff, (360) 748-9286; Skamania County Sheriff, (360) 427-5047; Clark County Sheriff, (360) 699-2211.

REGULATIONS IN DETAIL

Administrative Closures: The monument has several areas where administrative closures are in effect to protect fragile natural features and ongoing scientific research, as well as provide for visitor safety. The volcano's crater is closed to all public entry. A climbing permit is required on the mountain's west, south, and east flanks above 4,800 feet elevation. Coldwater Ridge, Johnston Ridge, the Spirit Lake Basin, and the Upper North Fork Toutle River Valley are closed to overnight camping, off-trail travel, pets, campfires, and stock use. When it opens, the Mount Margaret Backcountry will be managed as a distinct area where camping is by permit in designated sites only.

Use Quotas: Overnight use of the Mount Margaret Backcountry will be restricted in late 1998 with a ceiling of 44 visitors per night at 11 camp areas. Seasonal quotas for climbing Mount St. Helens (above 4,800 feet) also exist, currently restricted to 100 climbers per day, between May 15 and October 31 (60 advance permits, which may be reserved by mail, and 40 day-of-climb permits distributed by lottery). Climbing permits and registration are required year round. The following trails are heavily used: Lakes, Coldwater, Independence Pass, Harmony, Truman, Lava Canyon, Ape Cave, Ptarmigan, Boundary, Ape Canyon, Sheep Canyon, and Butte Camp.

Permit Requirements: Beginning in late 1998, use permits will be required for camping in the Mount Margaret Backcountry, with a ceiling of 44 visitors per night. For more information, call (360) 247-3900. Year-round permits and registration are required to climb Mount St. Helens above 4,800 feet to the rim. Restricted to 100 climbers per day (see "Use Quotas" and "Getting Permits").

Getting Permits: Up to 60 climbing permits per day are reservable from Monument Headquarters. Reservations are presently accepted by mail or in person beginning February 1, 1998, for the 1998 quota season (May 15–October 31). Up to 40 permits per day are available at Jack's Restaurant and Store on Highway 503, 22 miles east of I-5. When demand exceeds supply, these permits are distributed in a lottery system. You can enter the lottery between 5:30–6:00 P.M. on the day before you climb. The lottery is conducted promptly at 6:00 P.M., enabling climbers to get an early start the next morning. A per-person climbing permit fee of $15 was initiated in 1997 (not required November 1 through March 31). An annual pass, valid January 1, 1998 through December 31, 1998, costs $30. Be sure to call the Climbing Information Line at (360) 247-3961 for the most current information. It has not yet been determined where camping permits for the Mount Margaret Backcountry will be available. The camping permit fee will be $10 per site per night.

User Fee: A Monument Pass is required for designated developed sites within the National Monument (which includes the visitor center complexes, viewpoints, and interpretive sites. A Monument Pass valid for three consecutive days is $8. An annual pass is

$16 ($8 for seniors), children 15 and under free.

Backcountry Camping: Some areas of the monument are closed to all camping. Other areas such as the Mount Margaret Backcountry are open to camping by permit and in designated sites only. Still other portions of the monument are open to off-trail travel and dispersed camping. Campfires are not allowed in the blast zone (blown-down and standing dead forest).

Party Size: Climbing permit party size is limited to 12 for reserved permits and 4 for permits obtained through the unreserved permit lottery. Beginning in late 1998, both the number of parties per designated campsite and party size will be restricted in the Mount Margaret Backcountry. Limits vary with each site. For more information, contact Monument Headquarters.

▶ Special Issues: Visitors should remember that Mount St. Helens is still active and certain areas are subject to closure at any time for safety reasons. Check with Monument Headquarters or information centers for up-to-date information about access and volcanic activity. Note also that many roads in the monument become impassable in winter. Call (360) 247-3900 before departure.

Restrictions: Campfires: Prohibited within the blast zone (blown-down and standing dead forest). When critical fire conditions exist, stoves and smoking may also be prohibited.

Dogs: Dogs are prohibited on trails within the administrative closure area. Pets are also prohibited on designated interpretive trails throughout the monument and at the following trailheads and viewpoints on State Highway 504: Elk Bench, Lakes, Hummocks, South Coldwater, and Loowit. At Coldwater Ridge Visitor Center, Coldwater Lake Recreation Area, and Johnston Ridge Observatory pets are restricted to the designated pet areas. Where allowed, pets must be leashed and under control by their owners. Due to lack of water and shade, owners are encouraged to leave pets at home.

Stock: Prohibited on trails within the blast zone and some segments of trail that pass from green forest through the blast zone and back. For more information, contact Monument Headquarters.

Mountain Bikes: Allowed on monument trails, except within the administrative closure areas, the Mount Margaret Backcountry, and designated interpretive trails.

Motorized Vehicles: May be used only on roads, except for snowmobiles in designated areas.

Natural Resources: Pumice, ash, plants, and other natural and cultural features are protected and may not be removed.

Research Sites: Disturbance of research sites is prohibited.

27. Trapper Creek Wilderness

Administered by the U.S. Forest Service

LOCATION: Wind River area north of Stevenson in Skamania County.

GENERAL DESCRIPTION: Located southwest of Indian Heaven Wilderness in southern Washington, 6,050-acre Trapper Creek Wilderness protects the headwaters of Trapper Creek and its tributaries. It is adjoined by an additional 4,540 semi-primitive acres, which provide a further buffer from encroaching logging for the diverse wildlife that live here. Sister Rocks Research Natural Area, on the northwestern boundary of the wilderness, has been set aside for the study of subalpine forests and soils, with special emphasis on the Pacific silver fir.

GETTING THERE: From the southwest and southeast, take State Highway 14 east to Carson, then Forest Road 8C to Government Mineral Springs Campground and trailheads. From the east, use FR 30; from the west, FR 54.

NEW IN '98: Trail-Park Pass required for parking at trailheads (see "User Fee" summary on p. 7). To address the problem of increasing resource damage, the Gifford Pinchot National Forest is proposing a limited permit system for overnight backcountry use of wildernesses it manages. Some changes may take effect in the summer of 1998, with the limited permit system possibly beginning in 1999. Call ranger stations for the most up-to-date information.

REGULATIONS AT A GLANCE

User fee	Yes*
Wilderness permit required	Yes
Climbing permits and cards	No
Permit fee	No
Permit reservations available	No
Use quotas	No
Party size limit (combined people and stock)	12

*Trail-Park Pass required for parking at trailheads (see "User Fee" summary on p. 7).

ROADSIDE CAMPGROUNDS: The only campgrounds are Beaver Campground (24 sites, $) and Beaver Group Camp (maximum 75 people, $) near Government Mineral Springs. There is also limited camping in the vicinity of Government Mineral Springs. They are located just off FR 8C just outside the southern section of the wilderness. Reservable. Call (800) 280-CAMP.

NEAREST SERVICES: Carson has gas, food, and lodging.

RANGER DISTRICTS

❖ Gifford Pinchot National Forest, **Mt. Adams Ranger District,** Trout Lake (address/phone on p. 92)

❖ Gifford Pinchot National Forest, **Wind River Ranger District,** Carson (address/phone on p. 92)

Information, books, trail guides, permits, and maps available.

EMERGENCY CONTACTS: 911.

REGULATIONS IN DETAIL

Use Quotas: May be enacted in 1998.

Permit Requirements: Wilderness use permits are required for day and overnight trips.

Getting Permits: Available free from ranger stations and trailheads.

User Fee: Trail-Park Pass required for parking at trailheads (see "User Fee" summary on p. 7).

Backcountry Camping: Permitted throughout the wilderness. Camp at least 100 feet from lakes and streams.

Party Size: Twelve (combined people and stock).

Restrictions: Campfires are permitted throughout the wilderness. Use an existing fire ring and dead and downed wood only. Dogs are permitted throughout the wilderness. Stock are prohibited on most trails in Trapper Creek Wilderness; however, they are allowed on Observation Peak (trails #132 and 132A). The first 1.2 miles of Trapper Creek Trail #192.1, which accesses the non-wilderness Dry Creek Trail #194, is open to stock, as is the Big Hollow Trail #158, which accesses Observation Peak from the east. Stock must be kept 200 feet from lakes and streams. Do not tie directly to trees. Use a highline, hobble, or moveable picket. Certified weed- and seed-free processed feed only. Caching is prohibited.

28. Juniper Dunes Wilderness

Administered by the Bureau of Land Management

LOCATION: In Franklin County, 15 miles northeast of Pasco, northwest of Pasco-Kahlotus Road.

GENERAL DESCRIPTION: This 7,140-acre wilderness area, designated in 1984, contains the largest sand dunes in Washington, ranging from 200 to 1,200 feet wide and up to 130 feet high. The dunes support various grasses and shrubs, as well as the state's largest grove of western juniper trees. Used by a variety of mammals, reptiles, and birds, especially birds of prey. Bird watching is a popular activity here.

GETTING THERE: Take Interstate 82 to Pasco, then north on Pasco-Kahlotus Road. The wilderness is surrounded by private farmlands. Because of the lack of legal access, visitors are encouraged to contact the regional BLM office in Spokane prior to visiting the area. Access is also sometimes denied due to extreme fire danger in summer.

REGULATIONS AT A GLANCE

User fee	No
Overnight backcountry use permit required	For groups
Day use permit required	No
Permit fee	No
Use quotas	No
Party size limit	No

ROADSIDE CAMPGROUNDS: Two campgrounds are available in Pasco: Arrowhead RV Park (20 tent sites, 59 RV sites) and Greentree RV Park (40 RV sites).

NEAREST SERVICES: Food, accommodations, and gas are available in Pasco.

RANGER DISTRICT

U.S. Department of the Interior
Bureau of Land Management, Spokane District
Border Resource Area
1103 North Fancher
Spokane, WA 99212-1275
(509) 536-1200

Information, trip planning, maps, booklets, and permits.

INFORMATION CENTER: None on site. A part-time ranger lives in Richland and patrols the site on horseback during weekends, holidays, and high-use times. For complete site information, contact the BLM office in Spokane.

EMERGENCY CONTACTS: 911; Franklin County Sheriff, (509) 545-3500; BLM Spokane District, (509) 536-1200.

REGULATIONS IN DETAIL

Permit Requirements: Permits are only required for organized camping and for hiking parties of 15 or more.

Getting Permits: Groups should call or write the BLM Spokane District office for permission to use the wilderness.

Backcountry Camping: Primitive camping throughout the wilderness. No designated sites, water, or toilets available. All travel is cross-country, on foot, or on horseback.

Party Size: No limit.

▶ **Special Issues:** Exercise caution in summer due to soaring temperatures. There are no drinking water sources, distinctive landmarks, or developed trails in the dunes. Several old jeep trails into the area remain, but automobiles are not permitted. Access to the wilderness may be denied by landowners at any time. Contact BLM in advance of your trip to secure up-to-date information on entering the area. Hikers looking for solitude should avoid Juniper Dunes on summer weekends, when off-road vehicle activity on adjacent lands may prove distracting.

Restrictions: There are few restrictions in this wilderness. Open campfires are discouraged and, as always, off-road vehicles are prohibited in the wilderness.

29. Salmo-Priest Wilderness

Administered by the U.S. Forest Service

LOCATION: Northeast corner of Washington State, Pend Oreille County.

GENERAL DESCRIPTION: Shoehorned into the northeastern corner of Washington, touching both Canada and Idaho, this 39,937-acre wilderness in the Northern Rockies encompasses two long ridges connected on the north by a divide and several 6,000-foot-plus peaks. The western side is adjoined by 13,737 roadless acres containing biologically significant wetlands and, on the Idaho side, 17,600 acres proposed as wilderness. The wilderness is prime habitat for endangered grizzly bears and gray wolves, as well as the last wild herd of woodland caribou in the United States.

GETTING THERE: The main access to this wilderness is from the Washington side. Take State Highway 31, County Road 9345, then many forest roads to trailheads. The following roads are closed seasonally to motorized traffic to protect wildlife: Crowell Ridge Access Road 2212–200 (August 15–November 20), Slate Creek Access Road #3155 (April 1–June 30), Jackson Creek and Hughes Fork Access Road 662 (April 15–June 30). In addition, there is limited roadside parking at both Crowell Ridge trailheads and at the Shedroof Divide trailhead at Pass Creek Pass.

REGULATIONS AT A GLANC

User fee	No
Overnight backcountry permit required	No
Day use backcountry permit required	No
Party size limit (combined people and stock)	12

ROADSIDE CAMPGROUNDS: *Southwest of the Wilderness:* Mill Pond (10 sites, $), East Sullivan Lake (38 sites, $), West Sullivan Lake (6 sites, $), and Noisy Creek (19 sites, $). Approximately half the sites in Sullivan Lake and Noisy Creek campgrounds are reservable. Call (800) 280-CAMP. The rest are on a first-come, first-served basis. There is one group camp, the Sullivan Lake Group Campground ($), accommodating up to 30 people. To reserve, call (800) 280-CAMP.

NEAREST SERVICES: Food and lodging at Metaline Falls, about 6 miles from the southwestern edge of the wilderness. Gas at Metaline, about 1.5 miles from Metaline Falls.

RANGER DISTRICTS

❖ Colville National Forest, **Sullivan Lake Ranger District,** Metaline Falls (address/phone on p. 92)

Information, trip planning, exhibits, maps, books, interpretive program on Saturday nights in summer at East Sullivan Lake Campground.

❖ **Priest Lake Ranger District**
HCR5 Box 207, 32.5 Mile Marker Highway 57
Priest Lake, ID 83856
(208) 443-2512

EMERGENCY CONTACTS: 911; Pend Oreille County Sheriff, (509) 447-4942.

REGULATIONS IN DETAIL

Permit Requirements: None.

Backcountry Camping: *Northward from Crowell Ridge Trail #515:* Party size limit is 8 people. Pack stock are prohibited. Developed campsites have been phased out by naturalizing them, and the area is now managed for "No Trace" camping only (see p. 13), which is permitted at distances greater than 100 feet from streams and lakes. The purpose of these regulations is to protect this fragile and primitive core of the wilderness and to restore specific areas where impacts have occurred.

Trailed Areas: Party size limit remains at 12 people and stock animals combined. Developed campsites adjacent to streams are likely to be restored or moved by the year 2000 in order to reduce sanitation concerns, reduce vegetation loss at campsites, and disperse users. When this restoration project is complete, all developed campsites will be at least 100 feet from water bodies.

Other Considerations: Campfires are permitted in the wilderness, but encouraged only in existing developed campsites with fire rings. Dogs are allowed, but should be controlled to avoid harassing wildlife. Stock animals are permitted on existing trails, but not in the backcountry area as described above. Keep stock at least 100 feet from water and use only processed feed. Do not tie stock to trees; use a highline, hobble, or moveable picket. Both black and grizzly bears roam through the Salmo-Priest. Follow the precautions listed in "Bear Essentials" on p. 27.

❯ **Special Issues:** The wilderness is prime habitat for threatened and endangered species, including grizzly bears, gray wolves, and woodland caribou. Bull trout, a sensitive species, are also found here. Wilderness regulations are subject to change to protect species habitat.

30. Wenaha-Tucannon Wilderness

Administered by the U.S. Forest Service

LOCATION: Southeastern corner of Washington in Columbia, Asotin, and Garfield Counties and Wallowa County, Oregon.

GENERAL DESCRIPTION: Located in the Northern Blue Mountains of southeastern Washington and northeastern Oregon, the 177,465-acre wilderness encompasses rugged basaltic ridges and outcroppings separated by deep canyons (elevation 2,000–6,401 feet). Set aside in 1978, the wilderness was once a game preserve and still supports one of the largest elk herds in the state (due to a "grandfather clause," hunting is permitted in season).

GETTING THERE: US Highway 12 and State Highway 129 and various improved and unimproved forest roads to trailheads. Access from Oregon is via several forest service roads along the Wenaha River, near Troy.

NEW IN '98: Trail-Park Pass required for parking at trailheads (see "User Fee" summary on p. 7).

REGULATIONS AT A GLANCE

User fee . . . . Yes*
Overnight backcountry use permit required . . . . .No
Day use permit required . . . . .No
Party size limit (people and stock combined) 18
*Trail-Park Pass required for parking at trailheads (see "User Fee" summary on p. 7).

ROADSIDE CAMPGROUNDS: Primitive camping (toilets but no running water) at Indian (4 sites), Mottet (4 sites), Goodman (8 sites), Elk Flats (10 sites), Teepee (6 sites), Teal Spring (10 sites), and Tucannon (13 sites). Groups of approximately 20 can be accommodated at the Panjab Trailhead.

NEAREST SERVICES: Dayton and Pomeroy have gas, food, and lodging. Gas, propane, pay phone, food, and RV hook-ups are available at The Last Resort convenience store on the main Tucannon Road.

RANGER DISTRICT AND INFORMATION CENTER

❖ Umatilla National Forest, **Pomeroy Ranger District** (address/phone on p. 94)

Information, trip planning, books, and maps are available.

EMERGENCY CONTACTS: 911; Columbia County Sheriff, (509) 382-2518; Asotin County Sheriff, (509) 243-4171; Garfield County Sheriff, (509) 843-3499.

REGULATIONS IN DETAIL

Permit Requirements: None.
User Fee: Trail-Park Pass required for parking at trailheads (see "User Fee" summary on p. 7).
Backcountry Camping: Prohibited within 75 feet of streams and rivers.
Party Size: 18 heads per party, people and stock combined.
▸ **Special Issues:** Big game hunting seasons are from mid-October through mid-November. Hikers may wish to avoid the wilderness during this time. The wilderness is also designated Critical Habitat for the threatened Snake River Basin chinook salmon and regulated to preserve habitat for the species.

Restrictions: Campfires are prohibited within 75 feet of streams and rivers. Dogs are permitted on trails. Stock are permitted on trails but may not be tethered overnight. They are prohibited within 75 feet of streams and rivers. Processed feed is suggested.

Access to Backcountry Areas by Public Transportation
—*Peter Clitherow*

Even without a car, it is possible to get to many backcountry trailheads using a little creativity. The bus alone will get you near a number of areas and the combination of bus and bike will get you to quite a few others. Most of the local buses in the Puget Sound area are equipped with racks holding two bicycles.

CENTRAL WESTERN CASCADES
Greyhound/Trailways (206-628-5508)

♦ Snoqualmie Pass: Scheduled service from downtown Seattle, Tacoma, Olympia, Everett, Bellingham, and Mt. Vernon to Ellensburg and points east. Stops at the visitor center at the pass en route.

♦ Stevens Pass: While there is no scheduled service here, it is possible to be dropped off by Greyhound buses heading to Leavenworth over the pass. No pickup however. Leavenworth and Wenatchee are served by Greyhound/Trailways daily.

GrayLines of Seattle (206-624-5813)

♦ Mt. Rainier (Paradise Visitors Center): A daily service departing from the Washington State Convention Center in Seattle and SeaTac Airport to Mt. Rainier, leaving in the morning, returning in the evening, can be used for access during the spring and summer months. For round trips returning on a different day, the fare is slightly higher.

♦ Mount St. Helens (Coldwater Ridge Visitors Center): Service on Tuesdays and Thursdays from June to August.

Rainier Overland (360-569-0851) and Rainier Shuttle (360-569-2331)

♦ Transportation to Mount Rainier NP from SeaTac Airport and drop-off/pick-up at trailheads for the Wonderland Trail during the summer. Call for details.

METRO (800-542-7876). Bike racks on all buses.

♦ North Bend: North and Middle Fork Snoqualmie trailheads are accessible by bike from the Seattle area via North Bend. The Little Si and old Mt. Si trailheads are about 20 minutes' walk from the end of the North Bend bus run. The weekend Seattle–North Bend run has been replaced by a bus from Issaquah to North Bend. There are now connections to Issaquah from Downtown Seattle and the U-district in addition to the Eastside.

♦ Issaquah: The foothills around Issaquah have frequent service from the Seattle area and good access from the downtown Issaquah and High Point trailheads.

The Outing Club (206-363-0859)

♦ Provides winter ski trips to popular cross-country destinations from Seattle, Bellevue, Lynnwood, and Federal Way. Also overnight outings to Mt. Baker and the Methow Valley.

NORTHWESTERN CASCADES
Community Transit (800-562-1375). Bike racks on all buses.
- Darrington/Oso: Service from Arlington and Everett. The Mt. Higgins and Whitehorse Mountain trailheads are still a 20–30 minute walk from the bus stops; bus/bike combinations are quite reasonable.
- Granite Falls: Service from Everett. (Access to the Mountain Loop trailheads is still distant from Granite Falls; a bike and time will be needed.)
- Gold Bar, Sultan, and Startup: Service from Everett via Monroe; Wallace Falls trailhead is within walking distance of the bus stop in Gold Bar.

Ross Lake Water Taxi (206-386-4437)
- Ross Lake Trailheads: from Memorial Day weekend through the end of October, the water taxi (operated by Ross Lake Resort) can be used to access the northeast side of North Cascades NP and the Pasayten Wilderness via Ross Lake. Advance reservations advised for round trip or one way pick-up or drop-off.

EASTERN CASCADES
LINK (Chelan county buses) (509-662-1155). Bike racks for four in summer, ski racks in winter.
- Chelan/Entiat: Service from Wenatchee (except Sunday).
- Plain/Lake Wenatchee: Service from Leavenworth (except Sunday).
- Bluett Pass road (US 97): Service from Wenatchee and Leavenworth as far as the Ingalls Creek trailhead.
- Mission Ridge: A ski bus operates from Wenatchee to the ski area in winter.

Lake Chelan Boat Company (509-682-2224)
- Stehekin/Lucerne: Service twice daily in summer, less often in winter, from Chelan, also stopping at trailheads along the lake upon request (small extra charge for bicycles). See "Getting There" in the Glacier Peak Wilderness section on p. 43 for details.

North Cascades NPS bus (360-856-5703)
- Stehekin Valley: from Stehekin to trailheads as far as High Bridge. (Possibly Cottonwood by the end of summer 1998.) Call for the schedule. See "Getting There" in the Glacier Peak Wilderness section on p. 43 for details.

Holden Village Bus (no phone)
- Holden: bus service from Lucerne meets the *Lady of the Lake* in summer and the *Lady Express* in winter. Reservations advised at least two weeks in advance. See "Getting There" in the Glacier Peak Wilderness section on p. 43 for details.

Chelan Airways (509-682-5555)
- Stehekin/Lucerne: 30-minute floatplane ride up the lake from Chelan.

Methow Valley Ski Touring Association (MVSTA) 800-422-3048
- Methow Valley: In the winter, MVSTA operates a bus service picking up at points along the ski trail between Mazama and Winthrop.

OLYMPIC PENINSULA
Kitsap Transit (800-501-7433)
Mason Transit (800-374-3747)
Jefferson Transit (800-773-7788 East) (800-436-3950 West)
Clallam Transit (800-858-3747)
Bike racks on all buses.

◆ Olympic Peninsula: Kitsap, Mason, Jefferson, and Clallam Counties have linked their bus services together, so if you don't mind waiting, it's possible to travel US 101 all the way around the peninsula. However, in most cases the trailheads are some miles up a forest service road from the highway. Sequim, Port Angeles, Poulsbo, and Forks are the linking towns for bus services.

Olympic Van Tours/Olympic Bus Lines (800-550-3858)

◆ Port Angeles and northern Olympic Peninsula: Bus trips from Port Angeles to Hurricane Ridge and the Hoh rain forest.

◆ Backpacker Shuttle: To trailheads in the north Olympic Peninsula; e.g., Elwha, Sol Duc, Hoh River trailheads. This is a charter service based on hours of travel from Port Angeles. Available year round. Connecting direct bus service from downtown Seattle and SeaTac Airport.

The Ten Essentials

Carry these items with you whenever you travel into the backcountry:

1. Extra clothing—more than what you'd need in good weather.
2. Extra food—enough so some is left over at the end of your trip.
3. Sunglasses—necessary for most alpine travel and indispensable on snow.
4. Knife—for first aid and emergency fire building (making kindling).
5. Fire starter—a candle or chemical fuel for starting an emergency fire with wet wood.
6. First-aid kit.
7. Matches—stored in a waterproof container.
8. Flashlight—with spare bulb and batteries.
9. Map—make sure it's the right one for the trip.
10. Compass—know how to use it, and know the declination, east or west.

Other important items:

Water, water treatment, sunscreen, toilet paper, space blanket, whistle.

WASHINGTON'S 100 HIGHEST PEAKS

by the BULGER RULES (By John Lixvar and John Plimpton)

Rank Bulger List	Name	Height (ft)	Prom	USGS 7.5' Quad
1	Mount Rainier	14410	13210	Mount Rainier W
2	Mount Adams	12276	8116	Mount Adams E
3	Little Tahoma	11138	858	Mount Rainier E
4	Mount Baker	10781	8881	Mount Baker
5	Glacier Peak	10520+	7516	Glacier Peak East
6b	Mt. Saint Helens	9677b	5917	Mount St. Helens
6	Bonanza Peak	9511	3711	Holden
7	Mount Stuart	9415	5359	Mount Stuart
8	Mount Fernow	9249	2811	Holden
9	Mount Goode	9200+	3800	Goode Mountain
10	Mount Shuksan	9131	4411	Mount Shuksan
11	Buckner Mountain	9112	3032	Goode Mountain
12	Seven-Fingered Jack	9100	380	Holden
13	Mount Logan	9087	1487	Mount Logan
14	Jack Mountain	9066	4211	Jack Mountain
15	Mount Maude	9040+	842	Holden
16	Mount Spickard	8979	4779	Mt Spickard
17	Black Peak	8970	3450	Mount Arriva
18	Mount Redoubt	8969	1649	Mount Redoubt
19	Copper Peak	8964	484	Holden
20	North Gardner Mountain	8956	3479	Silverstar
21	Dome Peak	8920+	3040	Dome Peak
22	Gardner Mountain	8898	698	Mazama
23	Boston Peak	8894	854	Cascade Pass
24	Silver Star Mountain	8876	2436	Silver Star Mtn
25	Eldorado Peak	8868	2188	Eldorado Peak
26	Dragontail Peak	8840+	1760	Enchantment Lks
27	Forbidden Peak	8815	1055	Forbidden Peak
28	Mesahchie Peak	8795	2235	Mount Logan
29	Oval Peak	8795	2731	Oval Peak
30	Fortress Mountain	8760+	1680	Suiattle Pass
31	Mount Lago	8745	3268	Mount Lago
32	Robinson Mountain	8726	1686	Robinson Mtn
33	Colchuck Peak	8705	665	Enchantment Lks
34	Star Peak	8690	1170	Oval Peak
35	Remmel Mountain	8685	4376	Remmel Mountain
36	Katsuk Peak	8680+	440	Mount Logan
37	Sahale Peak	8680+	80	Cascade Pass

38	Cannon Mountain	8638	838	Cashmere Mtn
39	Mount Custer#	8630	1230	Mount Spickard
40	Ptarmigan Peak	8614	894	Mount Lago
41	Sherpa Peak	8605	405	Mount Stuart
42	Clark Mountain	8602	1522	Clark Mountain
43	Cathedral Peak	8601	961	Remmel Mtn
44	Kimtah (Gendarmes#) Peak	8600+	1040	Mount Logan
45	Mount Carru	8595	955	Mount Lago
46	Monument Peak	8592	1072	Mount Lago
47	Cardinal Peak	8590	2070	Pyramid Mtn
48	Osceola Peak	8587	1147	Mount Lago
49	Raven Ridge	8580e	1100	Martin Peak
50	Buck Mountain	8528+	1888	Clark Mountain
51	Storm King	8520+	600	Goode Mtn
52	Enchantment Peak	8520e	480	Enchantment Lks
53	Reynolds Peak	8512	2032	Sun Mountain
54	Primus Peak	8508	828	Forbidden Peak
55	Dark Peak	8504	264	Agnes Mountain
56	Mox Peaks (SE Twin Spire#)	8504	904	Mount Redoubt
57	Cashmere Mountain	8501	1581	Cashmere Mtn
58	Martin Peak	8500+	2100	Holden
59	Klawatti Peak	8485	685	Forbidden Peak
60	Horseshoe Peak	8480+	80	Cascade Pass
61	Mount Rahm	8480+	280	Mount Spickard
62	Big Craggy Peak	8470	3070	Billy Goat Mtn
63	Hoodoo Peak	8464	424	Hoodoo Peak
64	Lost Peak	8464	1624	Lost Peak
65	Chiwawa Peak	8459	1219	Suiattle Pass
66	Argonaut Peak	8453	733	Mount Stuart
67	Tower Mountain	8444	2884	Washington Pass
68	Dorado Needle	8440+	800	Eldorado Peak
69	Mount Bigelow	8440+	760	Martin Peak
70	Little Annapurna	8440+	280	Enchantment Lks
71	Sinister Peak	8440+	800	Dome Peak
72	Emerald Peak	8422	742	Saska Peak
73	Dumbell Mountain	8421	1261	Holden
74	NE Dumbell Mountain#	8415	655	Holden
75	Mox Peaks (NW Twin Spire#)	8407	527	Mount Redoubt
76	Saska Peak	8404	644	Saska Peak
77	Azurite Peak	8400+	1880	Azurite Peak
78	Luahna Peak#	8400+	720	Clark Mountain
79	Pinnacle Mountain	8400+	1720	Pinnacle Mountain
80	Blackcap Mountain	8397	397	Mount Lago
81	Courtney Peak	8392	792	Oval Peak
82	South Spectacle Butte	8392	1072	Holden
83	Martin Peak	8375	855	Martin Peak

84	Lake Mountain	8371	811	Mount Lago
85	Golden Horn	8366	1126	Washington Pass
86	West Craggy Peak	8366	686	Billy Goat Mtn
87	Mt. Saint Helens	8365	4605	Mount St. Helens
88	McClellan Peak	8364	1244	Enchantment Lks
89	Devore Peak	8360+	1722	Mount Lyall
90	Amphitheater Mountain	8358	758	Remmel Mountain
91	Snowfield Peak	8347	2907	Diablo Dam
92	Austera Peak	8334	414	Forbidden Peak
93	Windy Peak	8333m	1771	Horseshoe Basin
94	Cosho Peak	8332	492	Mount Logan
95	Big Snagtooth	8330+	570	Silver Star Mtn
96	Mount Formidable	8325	1885	Cascade Pass
97	Abernathy Peak	8321	801	Gilbert
98	Switchback (Cooney#) Mtn	8321	441	Martin Peak
99	Tupshin Peak	8320+	1080	Stehekin
100	Mount Flora	8320	1800	Pinnacle Mountain

Notes

b	Elevation and rank of Mount St. Helens before May 18, 1980 blast
#	Unofficial name, not on USGS map
e	Errors on 7.5' quads: *Ballard:* True summit is 0.2 miles SSE and ~40 feet higher than 8301' elevation shown on map; *Enchantment:* True summit is east peak shown as 8480+ contour; *Raven Ridge:* High point may be 8572' east summit
m	Elevation is calculated from metric map
Prom	Prominence is the elevation difference between a peak and the lowest contour that encircles it and no higher point.

A generation ago, in the mid-1970s, The Bulgers, an unconventional group of dedicated climbers, developed a list, and targeted climbing the 100 Highest Peaks in Washington, finishing in the 1980s and 1990s. The gold-standard chosen to define a peak for this list was "the 400-foot rule." The peak must unquestionably rise 400 feet above the saddle that separates it from the next higher peak. Mountains with this amount of prominence look like distinct summits in real life.

Some peculiarities to the "clean" 400-foot rule were introduced to the Bulger list: volcano-related summits with less than 800 feet of prominence were eliminated (Liberty Cap, 14,112'; Sherman Peak, 10,160'; Colfax Peak, 9,440'; and Lincoln Peak, 9,080;) and high summits named on the map, that had less than 400 ft. prominence, were added (Seven-fingered Jack, Sahale, Dark, Horseshoe, Rahm, Little Annapurna, and Black Cap). John Roper has been trying to popularize a "clean 400-foot Rule Top 100" list which cleans up the above mentioned peculiarities in the Bulger List (and adds Mount Ballard after Snowfield Peak—as it's actually 40 feet higher than the 8301' listed on the map—and Lone Peak, 8,311' at position 100).

At the end of 1997, 14 climbers had finished the Bulger Top 100 List. They are, in order: Russ Kroeker (on 10/4/80), Bruce Gibbs, Bob Tillotson, Bette Felton, John Roper, John Lixvar, Silas Wild, Joe Vance, Dick Kegel, John Plimpton, Dave Creeden, Mike Bialos, Jeff Hancock, and Johnny Jeans.

Quick Reference Guide

SOME GENERAL USE PHONE NUMBERS

Emergency

Washington State Patrol ....911 or (800) 283-7808

Mountain Search and Rescue 911

Boating Search and Rescue Coast Guard ....(206) 217-6000

Forest Fires ....(800) 562-6010

Poison Control Center (Tacoma) ....(800) 542-6319

Washington State Patrol and Game Agent ....(360) 426-6674

Washington State Highway Dept. (to report trees down/slides) ....(360) 895-4753

Road and Pass Conditions

Washington State Department of Transportation (WSDOT)

Mountain Pass Info (October 15–April 15) ....(888) SNO-INFO (766-4636)

in Greater Seattle Metro Area ....(206) DOT-HIWY (368-4499)

Puget Sound Area Road and Pass Info ....(800) 695-ROAD (7623)

South Puget Sound/Olympic Peninsula ....(360) 357-2789

Southwest Washington ....(360) 663-9641

South Central Washington ....(509) 527-2510

Eastern Washington ....(509) 324-6015

Avalanche Hazard and Snow Information

Cascades and Olympics ....(206) 526-6677

Mt. Hood/North Oregon Cascades ....(503) 808-2400

I-90 Corridor Sno-Park Report ....(509) 656-2230

Sno-Park and Washington State Parks Information ....(800) 233-0321

Other Numbers

Seattle Times Info Line/Weather ....(206) 464-2000, ext. 9900

National Weather Service Forecast ....(206) 526-6087

Whitewater Hotline (April–November) ....(206) 526-8530

USGS Maps ....(800) USA-MAPS

RECREATION INFORMATION CENTERS

Outdoor Recreation Information Center (ORIC)

222 Yale Avenue North

REI Store

Seattle, WA 98109-5429

(206) 470-4060

"Your source for National Park and National Forest Information." A joint Forest Service and National Park Service office. If you need one source for information on hiking and camping in Washington, ORIC is it. Tues.–Fri.: 10:30 A.M.–7:00 P.M. Sat.: 9:00 A.M.–7:00 P.M. Sun.: 9:30 A.M.–6:00 P.M.

Earth Science/National Forest Information Center

904 West Riverside, Room 135
Spokane, WA 99201-1088
(509) 353-2574
Information on eastern Washington and Idaho.

Nature of the Northwest Information Center

800 NE Oregon Street, Room 177
(State Office Building)
Portland, OR 97232
(503) 872-2750
http://www.naturenw.org/
Billing itself as "your one-stop source for outdoor recreation and natural resource information." The best source of information on Oregon, with a full range of information on
Washington. Web site has links to Washington's National Forests and wildernesses (those
with Web sites), and many other useful sites as well.

ON-LINE INFORMATION: THE INTERNET

The Mountaineers' Home Page: *Book catalog, club information,* Access Guide *updates, and
links to other sites:* http://www.mountaineers.org

Washington Trails Association: *Database of and reports about USFS and NPS trails in
Washington. Volunteer opportunities with WTA's trail maintenance program:* http://www.wta.org/wta/

Nature of the Northwest: *Links to national parks, forests, and wilderness in Washington and
Oregon, with Trail-Park info and outlets, list of reservable campgrounds, and ranger district reports:*
http://www.naturenw.org/index.html

United States Forest Service: http://www.fs.fed.us/

USFS Pacific NW Region (WA and OR): *Links to region's national forest pages:*
http://www.fs.fed.us/rb/rbnf.htm

Colville National Forest: *Ranger district reports, seasonal info:* http://www.fs.fed.us/crnf/

Gifford Pinchot National Forest: *Excellent frequently updated site, with ranger district and recreation reports, and trail, road, map, permit, regulation, campground, and seasonal info:*
http://www.fs.fed.us/gpnf/

Mt. Baker–Snoqualmie National Forest: *Ranger district reports, seasonal info:*
http://www.wired.web.com/~mbs/

Okanogan National Forest: *Ranger district reports, seasonal info:* http://www.fs.fed.us/rb/oka/

Olympic National Forest: *Well-thought-out site, with trail, campground, regulation, ecosystem management, and ONF wilderness area info, recreation report, Trail-Park Pass ordering:*
http://www.olympus.net/onf/index.htm

Wenatchee National Forest: *Ranger district reports, seasonal info:*
http://www.naturenw.org/forest/wen/index.html

National Park Service: http://www.nps.gov/

Mt. Rainier National Park: *Excellent site, with extensive, up-to-date trail and road reports, list of
trailside camps, recreation info, and more:* http://www.nps.gov/mora/mora.htm

North Cascades National Park: *General information about the Park:*
http://www.nps.gov/noca/

Olympic National Park: *Fairly extensive general information about the Park:*
http://www.nps.gov/olym/

Leave No Trace: *Minimum-impact wilderness techniques and links:* http://www.lnt.org/

National Outdoor Leadership School (NOLS): http://www.nols.edu/nols.html

Northwest Avalanche Center: *Vital avalanche danger and condition reports, mountain weather, and links to other avalanche and weather sites:* http://www.nwac.noaa.gov/

The Cyberspace Snow and Avalance Center: http://www.csac.org/

Natural Resources Conservation Snowpack Reports:
http://www.ocs.orst.edu/pub_ftp/weather/snow_reports/

Washington State Department of Transportation: *Mountain pass reports, Snoqualmie Pass camera, Seattle freeway traffic flow maps, weekly highway construction updates, ferry schedules:* http://www.wsdot.wa.gov/

National Weather Service, Seattle: http://www.seawfo.noaa.gov/

Washington Weather: http://www.nimbus.org/jumpstation/washington.html

Washington State Parks: http://www.parks.wa.gov/

Wilderness on the World Wide Web: *Comprehensive list with links to wilderness relevant resources including news, area lists, policy, education, management, and advocacy:* http://www.forestry.umt.edu/people/borrie/wilderness/default.htm

The Mountainzone: *Entertaining site, with articles, reports, and info on climbing, hiking, snowboarding, skiing, mountain biking, photography:* http://www.mountainzone.com (for up-to-date ski area snow reports add: /snowreports/usa/WA/index.html)

Great Outdoors Recreation Pages (GORP) for Washington: *Information on forests, national parks, outdoor activities, etc.:* http://www.gorp.com/gorp/location/wa/wa.htm

Backcountry Home Page: *Various interesting, entertaining, and often useful bits of information related to backcountry travel:* http://www.flash.net/~bhphiker/BHP/

Information on Washington Backcountry

WASHINGTON NATIONAL PARKS AND MONUMENTS
Olympic National Park

Visitor Center and Wilderness Information Center (WIC) . . . .(360) 452-0330
Eagle (Sol Duc) R.S. . . . .(360) 327-3534
Elwha R.S. . . . .(360) 452-9191
Heart O' the Hills R.S. . . . .(360) 452-2713
Hoh Rain Forest R.S. . . . .(360) 374-6925
Hoh Rain Forest Visitor Center . . . .(360) 374-6925
Kalaloch R.S. . . . .(360) 962-2283
Lake Crescent R.S. . . . .(360) 928-3380
Mora R.S. . . . .(360) 374-5460
Ozette R.S. . . . .(360) 963-2725
Queets R.S. . . . .(360) 962-2283
Quinault R.S. . . . .(360) 288-2444
Soleduck (Forks) R.S. . . . .(360) 374-6522
Staircase R.S. . . . .(360) 877-5569
Internet . . . . .http://www.nps.gov/olym/

North Cascades National Park/Ross Lake and Lake Chelan NRA

Park Headquarters . . . .(360) 856-5700, ext. 515
Glacier Public Service Center . . . .(360) 599-2714
Golden West Visitor Center (Stehekin) . . . . .(360) 856-5700, ext. 340/341 then 14

North Cascades National Park/Ross Lake and Lake Chelan NRA (cont.)

Wilderness Information Center in Marblemount . . . .(360) 873-4500, ext. 39
North Cascades Visitor Center in Newhalem . . . .(206) 386-4495, ext. 10
Stehekin R.S. . . . .(360) 856-5700, ext. 340/341
Internet . . . . .http://www.nps.gov/noca/

Mt. Rainier National Park

Park Headquarters . . . .(360) 569-2211
Wilkeson (Carbon River) R.S. (summer only) . . . .(360) 829-5127
Longmire Hiker Info Center . . . .(360) 569-2211, ext. 3317
Longmire R.S. . . . .(360) 569-2211, ext. 3305
Nisqually R.S. . . . .(360) 569-2211, ext. 2390
Ohanapecosh Visitor Center (summer only) . . . .(360) 494-2229
Paradise Info Center . . . .(360) 569-2211, ext. 2328
Paradise R.S. . . . .(360) 569-2211, ext. 2314
Sunrise R.S./Visitor Center (summer only) . . . .(360) 663-2425
White River RS/Wilderness Info Center (summer only) . . . .(360) 663-2273
Internet . . . . .http://www.nps.gov/mora/mora.htm

Mount St. Helens National Volcanic Monument

Headquarters . . . .(360) 247-3900
Mount St. Helens Visitor Center . . . .(360) 274-2100
Coldwater Ridge Visitor Center . . . .(360) 274-2131
Johnston Ridge Visitor Center . . . .(360) 274-2140

OTHER WASHINGTON AGENCIES AND NUMBERS

U.S. Fish and Wildlife . . . .(360) 753-9467

Yakama Indian Nation

Forest Development Office . . . .(509) 865-5121, ext. 657

Bureau of Land Management

Spokane Office . . . .(509) 536-1200

Columbia River Gorge National Scenic Area . . . .(541) 386-2333

Mt. Baker–Snoqualmie National Forest

Glacier Public Service Center . . . .(360) 599-2714
Snoqualmie Pass Visitor Center . . . .(425) 434-6111
Verlot Public Service Center . . . .(360) 691-7791

National Forest Headquarters

Colville NF . . . .(509) 684-7000
Gifford Pinchot NF . . . .(360) 891-5000
Mt. Baker–Snoqualmie NF . . . .(425) 775-9702
Wilderness Hotline (in Seattle use above number) . . . .(800) 627-0062
Okanagon NF . . . .(509) 826-3275
Olympic NF . . . .(360) 956-2400
Wenatchee NF . . . .(509) 662-4335

Volunteer Trailwork Coalition

(work parties, training) . . . .(206) 464-1641
Outside Seattle local calling area only . . . .(800) 650-1641

WASHINGTON WILDERNESS DIRECTORY

Wilderness	Forest	District	Phone
Alpine Lakes	Mt. Baker–Snoq.	Skykomish	(360) 677-2414
		North Bend	(425) 888-1421
	Wenatchee	Cle Elum	(509) 674-4411
		Leavenworth	(509) 548-6977
		Lk. Wenatchee	(509) 763-3103
Boulder River	Mt. Baker–Snoq.	Darrington	(360) 436-1155
Brothers	Olympic	Hood Canal	(360) 877-5254
Buckhorn	Olympic	Quilcene	(360) 765-2200
Clearwater	Mt. Baker–Snoq.	White River	(360) 825-6585
Colonel Bob	Olympic	Quinault	(360) 288-2525
Glacier Peak	Mt. Baker–Snoq.	Darrington	(360) 436-1155
		Mt. Baker	(360) 856-5700
	Wenatchee	Lk. Wenatchee	(509) 763-3103
		Entiat	(509) 784-1511
		Chelan	(509) 682-2576
Glacier View	Gifford Pinchot	Packwood	(360) 494-0600
Goat Rocks	Gifford Pinchot	Packwood	(360) 494-0600
	Wenatchee	Naches	(509) 653-2205
Henry M. Jackson	Mt. Baker–Snoq.	Skykomish	(360) 677-2414
		Darrington	(360) 436-1155
	Wenatchee	Lk. Wenatchee	(509) 763-3103
Indian Heaven	Gifford Pinchot	Mt. Adams	(509) 395-3400
Juniper Dunes	BLM	Spokane	(509) 536-1200
Lake Chelan–Sawtooth	Wenatchee	Chelan	(509) 682-2576
	Okanogan	Twisp	(509) 997-2131
		Winthrop	(509) 996-4000
Mt. Adams	Gifford Pinchot	Mt. Adams	(509) 395-3400
Mt. Baker	Mt. Baker–Snoq.	Mt. Baker	(360) 856-5700
Mt. Skokomish	Olympic	Hood Canal	(360) 877-5254
Noisy-Diobsud	Mt. Baker–Snoq.	Mt. Baker	(360) 856-5700
Norse Peak	Mt. Baker–Snoq.	White River	(360) 825-6585
	Wenatchee	Naches	(509) 653-2205
Pasayten	Okanogan	Winthrop	(509) 996-4000
		Tonasket	(509) 486-2186
Salmo-Priest	Colville	Sullivan Lake	(509) 446-7500
	Idaho Panhandle	Priest Lake	(208) 443-2512
Tatoosh	Gifford Pinchot	Packwood	(360) 494-0600
Trapper Creek	Gifford Pinchot	Wind River	(509) 427-3200
W. O. Douglas	Gifford Pinchot	Packwood	(360) 494-0600
	Wenatchee	Naches	(509) 653-2205
Wonder Mountain	Olympic	Hood Canal	(360) 877-5254

Washington National Forests
ADDRESSES AND PHONE NUMBERS

COLVILLE NATIONAL FOREST

Forest Headquarters
Colville National Forest
765 South Main
Colville, WA 99114
(509) 684-7000
http://www.fs.fed.us/cvnf/

Colville Ranger District
755 South Main
Colville, WA 99114
(509) 684-7010

Kettle Falls Ranger District
255 West 11th
Kettle Falls, WA 99141
(509) 738-7700

Newport Ranger District
315 North Warren
Newport, WA 99156
(509) 447-7300

Republic Ranger District
180 North Jefferson
Republic, WA 99166
(509) 775-3305

Sullivan Lake Ranger District
12641 Sullivan Lake Road
Metaline Falls, WA 99153
(509) 446-7500

GIFFORD PINCHOT NATIONAL FOREST

Forest Headquarters
Gifford Pinchot National Forest
10600 NE 51st Circle
Vancouver, WA 98682
(360) 891-5000
http://www.fs.fed.us/gpnf/

Mt. Adams Ranger District
2455 Highway 141
Trout Lake, WA 98650
(509) 395-3400
(509) 395-3422 (TDD)
(509) 395-3420 (weather info)

Packwood Ranger District
13068 US Highway 12
Packwood, WA 98361
(360) 494-0600

Randle Ranger District
10024 US Highway 12
Randle, WA 98377
(360) 497-1100

Wind River Ranger District
MP 23 Hemlock Road
Carson, WA 98610
(509) 427-3200

MOUNT ST. HELENS NATIONAL VOLCANIC MONUMENT HEADQUARTERS

42218 NE Yale Bridge Road
Amboy, WA 98601
(360) 247-3900

Mount St. Helens Visitor Center
3029 Spirit Lake Highway
Castle Rock, WA 98611
(360) 274-2100

Coldwater Ridge Visitor Center
3029 Spirit Lake Highway
Castle Rock, WA 98611
(360) 274-2131

MT. BAKER-SNOQUALMIE NATIONAL FOREST

Forest Headquarters
Mt. Baker–Snoqualmie National Forest
21905 64th Avenue W
Mountlake Terrace, WA 98043
(425) 775-9702
Wilderness Hotline: (800) 627-0062 (outside Seattle)
http://www.wired.web.com/~mbs/

Darrington Ranger District
1405 Emmens Street
Darrington, WA 98241
(360) 436-1155

North Bend Ranger District
42404 SE North Bend Way
North Bend, WA 98045
(425) 888-1421
(206) 622-8378 (Seattle line)

Mt. Baker Ranger District
2105 State Route 20
Sedro-Woolley, WA 98284-9394
(360) 856-5700

Skykomish Ranger District
P.O. Box 305
74920 NE Stevens Pass Highway
Skykomish, WA 98288
(360) 677-2414

White River Ranger District
857 Roosevelt Avenue E
Enumclaw, WA 98022
(360) 825-6585

Glacier Public Service Center
(summer only)
1094 Mt. Baker Highway
Glacier, WA 98244
(360) 599-2714

**Snoqualmie Pass Visitor
Information Center**
P.O. Box 17
Snoqualmie Pass, WA 98068
(425) 434-6111

Verlot Public Service Center
(summer only)
33515 Mountain Loop Highway
Granite Falls, WA 98252
(360) 691-7791

OKANOGAN NATIONAL FOREST

Forest Supervisor
Okanogan National Forest
1240 South Second Avenue
Okanogan, WA 98840
(509) 826-3275
http://www.fs.fed.us/rb/oka/

**Methow Valley Ranger District
Twisp Office**
P.O. Box 188
502 Glover Street
Twisp, WA 98856
(509) 997-2131

**Methow Valley Ranger District
Winthrop Visitor Center**
Highway 20, 1 West Winesap
Winthrop, WA 98862
(509) 996-4000

Tonasket Ranger District
P.O. Box 466
Tonasket, WA 98855
(509) 486-2186

OLYMPIC NATIONAL FOREST

Forest Headquarters
Olympic National Forest
1835 Black Lake Blvd. SW
Olympia, WA 98512-5623
(360) 956-2400
http://www.olympus.net/onf/index.htm

Hood Canal Ranger District
P.O. Box 68
150 North Lake Cushman Road
Hoodsport, WA 98548
(360) 877-5254

Quilcene Ranger District
P.O. Box 280
295142 Highway 101 South
Quilcene, WA 98376
(360) 765-2200

Quinault Ranger District
P.O. Box 9
353 South Shore Road
Quinault, WA 98575
(360) 288-2525

Soleduck USFS/NPS Ranger Station
196281 Highway 101
Forks, WA 98331
(360) 374-6522

UMATILLA NATIONAL FOREST

Forest Headquarters
Umatilla National Forest
2517 SW Hailey Avenue
Pendleton, OR 97801
(541) 278-3716

Pomeroy Ranger District
Route 1, Box 53-F
120 Main St.
Pomeroy, WA 99347
(509) 843-1891
(509) 843-4620

Walla Walla Ranger District
1415 West Rose Avenue
Walla Walla, WA 99362
(509) 522-6290

North Fork John Day Ranger District
P.O. Box 158
Ukiah, OR 97880
(541) 427-3231

Heppner Ranger District
P.O. Box 7
Heppner, OR 97836
(541) 676-9187

WENATCHEE NATIONAL FOREST

Forest Headquarters
Wenatchee National Forest
215 Melody Lane
Wenatchee, WA 98807-0811
(509) 662-4335
http://www.naturenw.org/forest/wen/index.
html

Cle Elum Ranger District
803 West Second Street
Cle Elum, WA 98922
(509) 674-4411

Chelan Ranger District
P.O. Box 189
428 West Woodin Avenue
Chelan, WA 98816
(509) 682-2576

Entiat Ranger District
P.O. Box 476
2108 Entiat Way
Entiat, WA 98822
(509) 784-1511

Lake Wenatchee Ranger District
22976 State Highway 207
Leavenworth, WA 98826
(509) 763-3103

Leavenworth Ranger District
600 Sherbourne Street
Leavenworth, WA 98826
(509) 548-6977

Naches Ranger District
10061 U.S. Highway 12
Naches, WA 98937
(509) 653-2205

Backcountry Support Organizations

Volunteers for Outdoor Washington
8511 15th Avenue NE, Room 206
Seattle, WA 98115
(206) 517-4469

Washington Trails Association
1305 Fourth Avenue, Suite 512
Seattle, WA 98101
(206) 625-1367, (800) 587-7032

Trail Team Hotline: (206) 517-7032
http://www.wta.org/wta/

Northwest Interpretive Association
909 First Avenue, Suite 630
Seattle, WA 98104-1060
(206) 220-4140

Washington Wilderness Coalition
4649 Sunnyside Avenue North, Suite 242
Seattle, WA 98103
(206) 633-1992

Backcountry Horsemen of Washington
11839 Glenwood Road SW
Port Orchard, WA 98367
(360) 876-7739

Volunteer Trailwork Coalition
530 SE Bush Street
Issaquah, WA 98027
(206) 464-1641
(800) 650-1641 (Outside Seattle local
area only)
vtc1@juneau.com

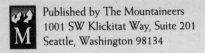 Published by The Mountaineers
1001 SW Klickitat Way, Suite 201
Seattle, Washington 98134

Manufactured in the United States

ISSN 1092-0358

Edited by Ken Lans
Map by Brian Metz
Cover design by Amy Peppler Adams, designLab
Book design by Alice Merrill
Layout by Peggy Egerdahl

♻ Printed on recycled paper

THE MOUNTAINEERS, founded in 1906, is a nonprofit outdoor activity and conservation club, whose mission is "to explore, study, preserve, and enjoy the natural beauty of the outdoors…" Based in Seattle, Washington, the club is now the third-largest such organization in the United States, with 15,000 members and five branches throughout Washington State.

The Mountaineers sponsors both classes and year-round outdoor activities in the Pacific Northwest, which include hiking, mountain climbing, ski-touring, snowshoeing, bicycling, camping, kayaking and canoeing, nature study, sailing, and adventure travel. The club's conservation division supports environmental causes through educational activities, sponsoring legislation, and presenting informational programs. All club activities are led by skilled, experienced volunteers, who are dedicated to promoting safe and responsible enjoyment and preservation of the outdoors.

The Mountaineers Books, an active, nonprofit publishing program of the club, produces guidebooks, instructional texts, historical works, natural history guides, and works on environmental conservation. All books produced by The Mountaineers are aimed at fulfilling the club's mission.

If you would like to participate in these organized outdoor activities or the club's programs, consider a membership in The Mountaineers. For information and an application, write or call The Mountaineers, Club Headquarters, 300 Third Avenue West, Seattle, WA 98119; (206) 284-6310.

Send or call for our catalog of more than 300 outdoor titles:
The Mountaineers Books
1001 SW Klickitat Way, Suite 201
Seattle, WA 98134
(800) 553-4453
e-mail: mbooks@mountaineers.org
website: www.mountaineers.org